CW00328994

GLORY DAYS

MASTRICK 23

LITTLEWOODS
£316.52l

284

Scottish Municipal Operators

Gavin Booth

Ian Allan PUBLISHING

1

CHOCOLATE! I want Cadburys!

48

CORPORATION TRANSPORT

Front cover: A typical one-man-operated Glasgow Atlantean (identifiable by the orange spot on the dome) seen in 1971 city-bound on a realigned section of Alexandra Parade on an experimental express service to Easterhouse. Behind is the former Monkland Canal, soon to become the M8 motorway.
Iain MacGregor

Back cover: Dundee Corporation favoured AEC and Daimler buses from the 1930s. At the Shore Terrace terminal point is a 1953 Daimler CVD6 with Weymann body, rebuilt by the corporation.
Campbell Sayers

Title page: Edinburgh and Aberdeen bought 'Pilcher' cars from Manchester Corporation. Aberdeen placed 14 in service in 1948/9, including No 48, seen at the Bridge of Dee terminus. These cars were built 1930-2 by Manchester Corporation on Peckham P35 trucks.
J. Copland / Photobus

Contents

First published 2003

ISBN 0 7110 2867 2

© Ian Allan Publishing Ltd 2003

Published by Ian Allan Publishing

an imprint of Ian Allan Publishing Ltd, Hersham, Surrey KT12 4RG.

Printed by Ian Allan Printing Ltd, Hersham, Surrey KT12 4RG.

Code: 0303/x

Introduction

Few readers will have first-hand experience of more than the four Scottish municipal transport fleets that survived into the 1970s. More than 40 years earlier there had been another five corporation undertakings that had joined the rush to build and operate tramways within their boundaries in the early part of the 20th century, and, while a couple moved on to motorbus operation, all had to face the reality that to upgrade track, overhead and rolling stock would be a costly business, and that the entrepreneurial new bus companies of the SMT Group offered a face-saving way out. In Kirkcaldy and Perth SMT even recognised the importance of retaining separately-liveried 'town service' fleets that would survive for almost 30 years.

In this book we look at all nine Scottish municipal transport operations, concentrating on the four that were by far the biggest, and have the longest and most distinguished histories. Although there were common strands, the corporation tram and bus undertakings at Aberdeen, Dundee, Edinburgh and Glasgow were all fiercely independent. Their managers met regularly through their trade organisation, the Scottish Road Passenger Transport Association, and compared notes. There were no competition issues in those days, and the municipal managers sat down with their opposite numbers from the SMT Group companies to discuss matters of mutual interest and concern.

The municipal managers no doubt compared notes on recent trends, and would take every opportunity to show off their latest acquisition, maybe a new tram or bus. But there is little sign that they allowed themselves to be influenced by their peers, and continued to plough their own furrows. There was little similarity in their tramcar policies, for instance. All had their own design of standard car, usually built in their own workshops, and, while Dundee bought no new cars after 1930, Aberdeen bought no new cars between 1931 and 1940, when it invested in four impressive streamliners, and bought 20 more in 1949. Edinburgh came late to electric trams, in 1922, and added new cars to the fleet on a regular basis until 1950 — all rather staid four-wheelers. Glasgow found itself in the 1930s with a vast fleet of over 1,000 ageing four-wheel standard cars, and embarked on a massive programme of new building that produced the Coronation bogie cars, certainly among the most impressive double-deck trams built for use in Britain.

On the motorbus side there were stronger similarities. In each of the four cities the trams provided the core network right through to the 1930s, with buses acting initially as feeders to new residential and commercial developments. Some tramways were extended, but as the diesel bus became more reliable and attractive, the bus found itself playing an increasingly important role. After World War 2 new buses were bought in increasing numbers, but in the 1950s the trams were seen as costly to maintain and extend, and the bus was set to be the transport of the future.

Aberdeen and Dundee tended to favour AEC and Daimler buses for a number of years, while Glasgow shopped around more widely, and included locally-built Albions. Edinburgh went

▲ Glasgow was one of the pioneering operators of the then-revolutionary Leyland Atlantean, buying one of the four pre-production prototypes. LA1, with 78-seat Alexander body, was first shown at the 1958 Commercial Motor Show. *Ian Allan Library*

Glasgow's tramway system became legendary and is still fondly remembered by older Glaswegians. With a fleet of well over 1,000 trams at its height, it developed what were justly regarded as some of the finest passenger vehicles in Europe, the 'Cunarders'. *Photobus*

from prewar Daimlers to a postwar mixture that eventually settled on Leylands. Local bodybuilders were also favoured by the Scottish municipal fleets, but in the postwar period Metro-Cammell and Park Royal did well until Alexander, recently released from the SMT Group, got its act together and started selling into the four fleets in a very big way.

The other municipal operator that could almost be regarded as Scottish was Belfast, whose managers attended SRPTA meetings with their Scottish counterparts, and there is evidence of ideas flowing in both directions between Scotland and Northern Ireland — Belfast's McCreary tramcars, for instance, would not have looked out of place in Edinburgh.

In this book I have concentrated on what were arguably the glory days for the four big municipal fleets — the period from the late 1930s, when the tramway systems were reaching their peak, new and often exciting trams were being placed in service,

and truly modern buses with diesel engines and preselector gearboxes were replacing their cruder predecessors from the previous decade, right through to the 1970s, when local-government reorganisation placed the Aberdeen, Dundee and Edinburgh undertakings in regional control and Glasgow Corporation became the core of the new Greater Glasgow PTE. The days of true corporation-owned buses really ended then, and the original ethos — the desire to provide a quality service at affordable fares for the local citizens — was slightly lost when transport moved rather further into the political arena.

Scotland can be proud of its municipal transport undertakings. They served their public well, and this book is a tribute to the staff who worked hard to provide a truly public service.

Gavin Booth
Edinburgh
November 2002

The big Scottish municipal fleets supported local coach-builders. Sometimes these were based in the city itself, while others were found elsewhere in Scotland. Although Alexander became the bodybuilder of choice in the 1950s, companies such as Cowieson, based at St Rollox, Glasgow, were favoured before the war. This all-metal Cowieson body is mounted on a 1936 Dundee Corporation Daimler COG6, a chassis type selected by all four fleets. *Gavin Booth collection*

Metro-Cammell lost its Scottish business when Alexander started making inroads into the four Scottish municipalities. Two Aberdeen Daimler CVG6s provide a contrast between Metro-Cammell-bodied No 231 of 1957 and Alexander-bodied No 308 of 1963. The photograph also shows the two styles of Daimler 'tin front' — the Birmingham style on the left and the later Manchester style. *Photobus*

7

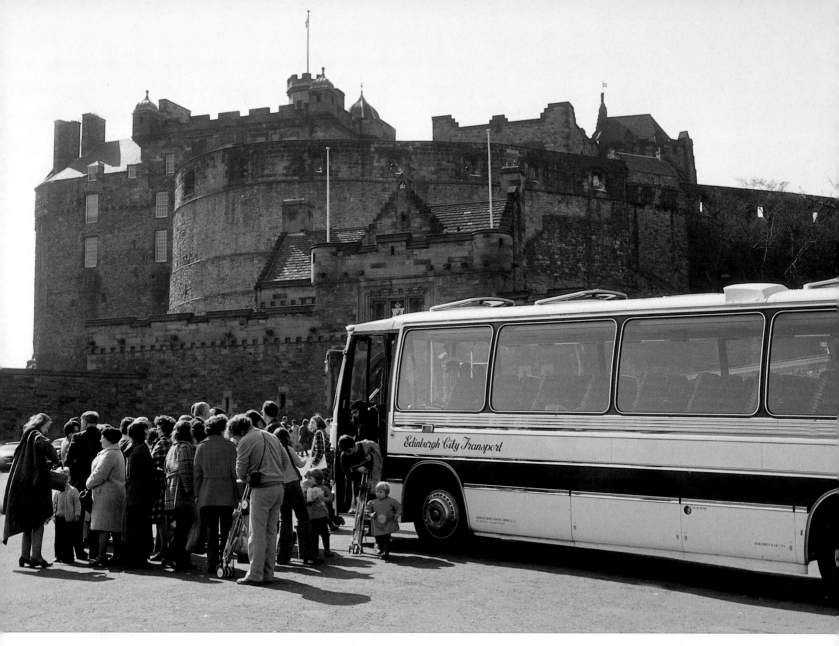

Coach touring was good business for Edinburgh Corporation since it first bought charabancs in 1919. Passengers unload from a Bedford YRT with Duple Dominant body on Edinburgh Castle Esplanade in April 1974. *Gavin Booth*

Like Glasgow, Edinburgh Corporation was interested in the idea of Continental-style standee-type single-deckers as an alternative to the predominant double-decker. It dabbled in the early 1950s with Royal Tigers and an Olympic, and again in 1961 with the famous three-door Leyland Leopard, No 101. By 1975 101 had been converted to a single-door 45-seater and was in use on normal bus duties, as here at Juniper Green. *Gavin Booth*

Scotland's Nine Municipal Fleets

The fact that there were just four Scottish municipal tram and bus fleets in the post-World War 2 years (out of roundly 100 in the UK, when Scottish residents represented roundly 10% of the UK population) is more to do with geography than any resistance to municipal ownership. Before the war the figure had been higher. In addition to Aberdeen, Dundee, Edinburgh and Glasgow, which survived into the 1970s with corporation fleets, there were municipal tram fleets at Ayr, Kirkcaldy and Leith, and tram/bus fleets at Kilmarnock and Perth, but Leith disappeared when that burgh reluctantly merged with Edinburgh in 1920, and the others decided to sell their undertakings to members of the fast-growing SMT Group in the 1930s.

Aberdeen, Dundee, Edinburgh and Glasgow have been Scotland's four biggest cities for many years now, and they are well spread throughout the country. Edinburgh and Glasgow are closest to each other — just 45 miles apart — and Aberdeen, some 60 miles north of Dundee, was the UK's most northerly municipal operator. As a result, the joint municipal operations that were a fascinating feature of areas like Manchester, South Wales and Yorkshire were never a part of the Scottish scene. There was some joint tramway operation involving the Scottish municipals, but this was with privately-owned companies. Where two separate municipal operations existed, as with Edinburgh and Leith, there was no through operation between the burghs

Glasgow came late to trolley-buses, in 1949, and they enjoyed brief popularity on routes that were often out of the public eye. TB113 is in St Vincent Place in July 1965 heading south on a short-working of service 105, which normally ran to Clarkston beyond the city boundary. These attractive BUT 9613S vehicles had Crossley/PRV bodies.
Iain MacGregor

Heavyweight underfloor-engined single-deckers were tried by Dundee, Edinburgh and Glasgow. This is a Dundee 1953 AEC Regal IV with Weymann body, uniquely converted to dual-door layout.
Photobus

Aberdeen Corporation resisted rear-engined double-deckers until 1967, when it bought 10 Leyland Atlantean PDR1/1 models with Alexander bodies, like No 120 seen in 1972. The letters EFB indicate Experimental Fare Box.
G. R. Mills

because, while Leith had opted for electric tramways, Edinburgh persisted with its anachronistic cable-driven system; only after the 1920 merger of the two burghs did common sense prevail and electric trams cover the expanded city of Edinburgh.

The combined populations of Aberdeen, Dundee, Edinburgh and Glasgow represent nearly one third of the Scottish total, and there is a gap before you reach the next group of large Scottish towns, which include East Kilbride, Paisley, and Motherwell & Wishaw. Thus each of the four municipalities was big enough to justify an important transport undertaking, operating trams and then buses and, in the case of Dundee and Glasgow, trolleybuses — though Dundee's were short-lived. In 1952, just past the postwar travel peak, Glasgow boasted the largest of the 96

municipal fleets in the UK, with over 2,000 buses, trams and trolleybuses. Edinburgh was seventh on the list, with 699 buses and trams, Aberdeen 17th, with 268, and Dundee 28th, with 209.

This meant that each of the four undertakings was big enough to go its own way on such matters as vehicle design, and Glasgow famously built most of its own trams right into the 1950s, and built bus bodies into the early 1960s. Aberdeen, Dundee and Edinburgh also built many of their own trams, and, although the bus-buying policies of the four had certain similarities, each was able to develop its own very individual style.

The tables showing fleet sizes on page 17 illustrate the dramatic growth that the four surviving Scottish municipal transport undertakings enjoyed in the 1930s. In the 1920s the

Aberdeen and Dundee tram fleets were still growing at a
reasonable pace, but the fleet totals were being boosted by
deliveries of new motorbuses. By 1937 Aberdeen's bus and tram
fleets were more-or-less equal, and Dundee's buses already
outnumbered its trams.

Edinburgh went more enthusiastically for motorbuses in the
1920s; between 1920 and 1929 the total fleet size almost doubled,
and by 1929 the tram fleet had almost reached its peak. The bus
fleet continued to grow in the 1930s and by 1937 represented
more than one third of the fleet.

Glasgow Corporation had no buses in 1920, but a vast and
highly-standardised fleet of 924 trams. By 1929 the tram total
was up to 1,143 and there were 152 buses. By 1937, although
new Coronation cars were beginning to arrive, the tram fleet had
been reduced to 1,093 and the bus fleet had grown to 532 —
nearly one third of the total.

The 1952 figures show the size of the four tramway fleets in
the last year before the withdrawal process got under way, with
Aberdeen's and Dundee's buses outnumbering their trams,
Edinburgh with an equal number of buses and trams, and only
Glasgow with a dominant tram fleet, although motorbuses and
the recently-introduced trolleybuses were fast catching up.
By 1959 buses outnumbered Glasgow's trams — but there
were still over 800 of these at the time.

The 1969 figures show that, apart from Dundee, which
managed to remain unchanged, the other three Scottish fleets
were down in number — a trend that would continue. Glasgow
had dropped most dramatically: 1,242 against the 1959 figure
of 1,918 — a 35% drop. Falling passenger numbers, coupled
with higher-capacity buses and more efficient operating
practices, mean that the equivalent fleets today are
considerably smaller.

Glasgow Corporation supported local industry by buying Albions in healthy numbers from 1935. Its last were 25 CX37SW models with Weymann bodies bought in 1953. B130 is seen in George Square.
Iain MacGregor

The Scottish municipal fleets, 1920

	Motorbuses	Tramcars	TOTAL
Aberdeen	4	94	98
Ayr	-	24	24
Dundee	-	82	82
Edinburgh	36	213	249
Glasgow	-	924	924
Kilmarnock	-	14	14
Kirkcaldy	-	26	26
Leith	-	37	37
Perth	3	12	15

The Scottish municipal fleets, 1929

	Motorbuses	Tramcars	TOTAL
Aberdeen	59	132	191
Ayr	-	24	24
Dundee	22	73	95
Edinburgh	130	357	487
Glasgow	152	1,143	1,295
Kilmarnock	18	-	18
Kirkcaldy	-	26	26
Perth	30	-	30

The Scottish municipal fleets, 1937

	Motorbuses	Tramcars	TOTAL
Aberdeen	104	109	213
Dundee	88	60	148
Edinburgh	193	360	553
Glasgow	532	1,093	1,625

The Scottish municipal fleets, 1952

	Motorbuses	Tramcars	Trolleybuses	TOTAL
Aberdeen	169	99	-	268
Dundee	153	56	-	209
Edinburgh	349	350	-	699
Glasgow	833	1,149	65	2,047

The Scottish municipal fleets, 1959

	Motorbuses	Tramcars	Trolleybuses	TOTAL
Aberdeen	236	-	-	236
Dundee	240	-	-	240
Edinburgh	713	-	-	713
Glasgow	971	806	141	1,918

The Scottish municipal fleets, 1969

	Motorbuses	TOTAL
Aberdeen	227	227
Dundee	240	240
Edinburgh	696	696
Glasgow	1,242	1,242

▲ Wartime deliveries to Aberdeen and Dundee were Daimler CWA6s that fitted well into the existing fleets. Three of Dundee's Brush-bodied examples are seen at Maryfield tram sheds. *courtesy Alan Brotchie*

▶▶ The Smaller Fleets

Five Scottish municipal transport operations disappeared before
World War 2. All had operated trams, and two had moved on to
motorbuses before they sold out to companies in the burgeoning
SMT Group.

Ayr

The first to start operation was Ayr Corporation Tramways, on
26 September 1901, with electric tramway services in Ayr and
the neighbouring burgh of Prestwick, on the Clyde coast. In 1902
the standard-gauge tramway was extended south to Alloway, and
in 1907 a branch was opened eastwards to the new racecourse.

Ten open-top double-deck trams were bought from Hurst Nelson
of Motherwell to open the system, and further cars arrived from
the same supplier until 1916; the two 1916 cars were new with
top covers and were the last new trams bought. Some of the older
cars received top covers in 1919 and vestibuled platforms in the
1920s. Subsequent purchases were bought second-hand — four
single-deckers from Manchester Corporation in 1922 and two
former Dumbarton double-deckers in 1928. The Ayr trams were
painted chocolate and primrose.

The Ayr trams suffered from the growth of motorbus
competition in the 1920s, and the seasonal nature of a system
serving this popular seaside town was a further complication.

An approach was made by the
Scottish Motor Traction (SMT)
company to buy the tramway
system and replace it with
motorbuses, and a deal was
concluded with Ayr Town
Council in November 1931.
The last tram ran on
31 December 1931, after which
SMT buses took over; although
the new Western SMT
company took over most of
SMT's interests in Ayrshire, the
Ayr and Prestwick locals
remained licensed to the
Edinburgh SMT company —
an anomaly that would survive
for some 30 years.

Like Ayr, Perth Corporation turned to Hurst Nelson for its cars — 12 open-top double-deckers — and these would be the only electric cars bought for the system. Not all were identical, however; three were to a slightly lower height, to operate under the railway bridge in King Street. The 'low' cars were painted olive green to distinguish them; the main fleet livery was lake and cream.

Perth Corporation was an early user of motorbuses and operated Scotland's first municipal example, a Bellhaven charabanc bought in 1911; other buses were bought over the next few years, mainly to provide services beyond the reach of the tramway, but competition from the Perth General Omnibus Co (from November 1927) hastened the end of the corporation's trams. A report recommended replacement by motorbuses, and the trams struggled on to the last day of operation, 19 January 1929. By this time Perth Corporation had over 30 motorbuses, including 11 from the Perth General company, acquired in August 1928.

From 1927 Thornycrofts were favoured, and the last new buses bought were two Thornycroft Daring double-deckers with Metro-Cammell bodies and two Crossley Condors with Pickering bodies. On 16 May 1934 the bus services were transferred to Walter Alexander & Sons, part of the SMT Group, which continued to run the Perth services in a red-and-cream livery with Perth City Transport fleetnames. The livery lasted until 1961, though the fleetname had disappeared in the early postwar years. Strathtay Scottish would resurrect the livery and fleetname for services competing with Stagecoach in 1989.

Perth Corporation No 5 from the original 1905 electric fleet built by Hurst Nelson, in Scone on the way to Cherrybank. The Scone depot is beyond the tram. The poor condition of the road surface explains the popularity of the tramcar in the early years of the last century. *courtesy Alan Brotchie*

Perth

The next Scottish burgh to operate trams was Perth, situated on the River Tay north of the central belt. There had been horse-bus services linking Perth with Scone, to the east, and these were taken over by the new Perth & District Tramways Co in 1894. Work was then started on building a 3ft 6in-gauge tramway between Perth and Scone, which was opened in September 1895, operated by a fleet of horse-drawn trams. Extensions were built within Perth in 1897/8.

Perth Town Council now sought to buy the Perth & District company, and Perth Corporation Tramways took over on 7 October 1903. Authority to electrify the system was obtained in 1904, and the last horse cars were replaced by electric cars on 31 October 1905.

▲ Perth abandoned its trams in favour of motorbuses in 1929, and among its last purchases before the system was taken over by W. Alexander & Sons in 1934 was this Thornycroft Daring with MCCW bodywork, one of two bought in 1933 along with two Crossley Condors. Alexanders used the name Perth City Transport on a proportion of the local fleet, and the livery and name were revived in the 1980s by Strathtay Scottish for a competitive venture. *Gavin Booth collection*

Kirkcaldy

The only electric tramway in Fife that was municipally-owned served Kirkcaldy, on the northern shores of the Firth of Forth. The two other Fife tramways were operated by the Dunfermline & District and Wemyss & District companies; the Wemyss trams, running along the coastal strip to the east of Kirkcaldy, joined with the Kirkcaldy system at Gallatown and ran over corporation tracks into the centre of the town.

The 3ft 6in-gauge Kirkcaldy system opened on 28 February 1903 using 10 open-top double-deck cars built by Milnes, painted in dark olive green and cream. Twelve more similar cars followed in 1903/4, and the last cars to be bought were four from Hurst Nelson in 1914.

The Wemyss tramway system opened in August 1906 and led to joint through running between Kirkcaldy and Leven.

The poor state of the Kirkcaldy tramway prompted the corporation to consider motorbuses and trolleybuses as replacements, but once more SMT stepped in, this time using its local company, Walter Alexander & Sons. An offer to buy the system was accepted, and the last trams ran on 15 May 1931.

SMT had already bought the Wemyss tramways, and these closed in January 1932. Alexanders, rather than its local subsidiary, General Motor Carrying, operated the buses replacing the Kirkcaldy trams and, as in Perth, the 'town service' buses wore a red-and-cream livery until 1961.

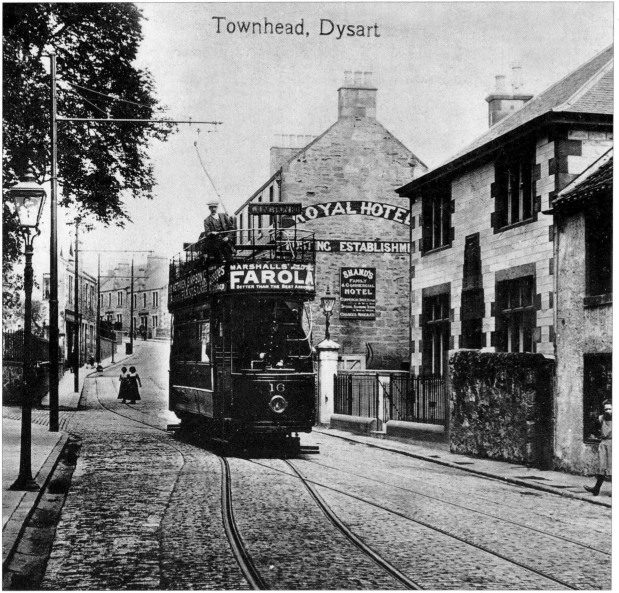

Townhead, Dysart

A fine streetscape at the Links terminus of Kirkcaldy Corporation, featuring No 17, a 1904 Milnes car, and a selection of the local youth. This was the western end of the town's tramway. The 3ft 6in track gauge is very evident. *E. O. Catford, courtesy Alan Brotchie*

The Kirkcaldy tramway was extended into the neighbouring burgh of Dysart in 1911. At the Dysart terminus is No 16, built in 1904 by Milnes. *courtesy Alan Brotchie*

Leith

Although Leith is now part of Edinburgh, until 1920 it was a separate burgh, and in 1904 it acquired the horse-tram services within its boundaries that had previously been operated by the Edinburgh Street Tramways company. The company's former horse-tram services in Edinburgh itself were being converted to cable operation at the time, but Leith resisted the cable system (sensibly, as it turned out) and decided to go for electric traction.

The Leith electric system opened on 18 August 1905 using trams from an initial order for 36 cars shared equally between UEC and Brush. All were double-deck, and all but six were open-toppers. Top covers were fitted to the open-top cars between 1912 and 1914. An 'instruction car' bought in 1906 was fitted with a Brush open-top body. The Leith cars were painted Munich Lake (dark red) and white.

With the amalgamation of Leith and Edinburgh in 1920, control of the Leith tramway system passed to Edinburgh Corporation's tramways department. The incompatibility of the Leith electric and Edinburgh cable systems had led to the 'Pilrig muddle', where passengers had to change trams at the boundary between the two burghs, in Leith Walk. This was resolved in 1922, when Edinburgh started to replace its cable cars with electric cars, and through running was possible for the first time since horse-tram days.

▲ Leith Corporation No 16, a 1905 Brush-built car, near the Foot of Leith Walk, the focal point for the burgh. To the right of the tram, the building with the clock tower is Leith Central station. With the other Leith cars No 16 gained a top cover and later passed into the Edinburgh Corporation fleet, surviving until 1933.
Gavin Booth collection

At Newhaven, on the Firth of Forth, Leith Corporation No 13 prepares to return to the boundary with Edinburgh at Pilrig. It is a 1905 car built by United Electric Car at Preston on Brill 21E truck. The horse bus on the right provided a link with Granton, to the west, whither the tramway was later extended. *courtesy Alan Brotchie*

25

▲ Kilmarnock Corporation operated just 14 cars, all built
by Hurst Nelson in 1904/5. No 1 is seen in Glencairn Square
in the early years of the Ayrshire system.
courtesy Alan Brotchie

Kilmarnock

Back in Ayrshire, Kilmarnock Corporation, possibly inspired by the example of nearby Ayr, decided to explore the construction of a standard gauge electric tramway system in the town. This opened on 10 December 1904 using 11 open-top double-deckers supplied by Hurst Nelson; a 12th example followed in 1905, and just two more cars were bought — top-covered double-deckers, again from Hurst Nelson, also in 1905. The trams were painted olive green and cream.

Like many small systems, the Kilmarnock trams did well in their earlier years, but the track and the fleet deteriorated, necessitating expensive repairs, and the situation was aggravated by the appearance of competing motorbuses; the competitor here

was the BET's Scottish General Transport company. In 1924 Kilmarnock Corporation decided to replace one of its tram services with buses. The first were Albion and Thornycroft single-deckers, and from 1924 to 1930 the undertaking bought a total of 22 buses. The success of these led to a decision to withdraw the remaining trams, which ran for the last time in May 1926.

An approach was made by SMT in 1931 to find out if the corporation would sell its bus operations. The SMT offer was accepted, and on 31 December 1931 — the same day as at nearby Ayr — municipal bus operation ceased in Kilmarnock. SMT took over, and the operation passed to the new Western SMT company in June 1932.

▲ This Albion PM28 with Northern Counties bodywork was bought by Kilmarnock Corporation in 1927 at a cost of £1,205. It passed to SMT with most of the municipal fleet at the end of 1931. *courtesy Alan Brotchie*

▲ Union Street is Aberdeen's
main thoroughfare. In this
postcard view from the early
years of the last century,
corporation trams Nos 27 and
33 head to the west of the city.
Built by the British Electric
Car Co in Manchester on Brill
21E trucks, they lasted until
the early post-World War 2
years. *Gavin Booth collection*

Aberdeen

North of Dundee and Scotland's central belt, Aberdeen is the
only city with a population comparable to Dundee, Edinburgh
and Glasgow. Its 1967 total of just over 182,000 ranked it (just)
behind Dundee; the next largest centre in the North was
Inverness, with barely one sixth of that figure. Situated on the
North Sea coast between the rivers Dee and Don, Aberdeen had
for several centuries been an important sea port and seat of
learning, until the arrival of the railways in 1850 sparked off a
significant change in the local economy. The city's population
grew dramatically in the 19th century, and it was inevitable that
horse buses and trams would be introduced.

The Aberdeen District Tramways Co opened its first lines
in 1874 and expanded over the next two decades. Aberdeen

Corporation purchased the company's assets in August 1898
and immediately started to electrify the system. The first electric
cars ran in December 1899, and within three years all the horse
trams had been replaced by electric cars. Routes operated to
Bayview, Bridge of Dee, Bridge of Don, Ferryhill, Kittybrewster,
Mannofield, Queen's Cross, Rosemount, Torry and Woodside.

Bus services to areas beyond the tramways started in 1921 and
developed steadily, and, while the Ferryhill and Torry tram routes
were abandoned in 1931, there were also tramway extensions —
to Hazlehead in 1924 and Scatterburn in 1938.

There was another electric tramway operator, Aberdeen
Suburban Tramways, which ran services beyond the city boundary
on the Deeside Road to Bieldside and on the Great Northern Road
to Bankhead. Opened in 1904, the AST system suffered badly
from pirate bus competition and closed in 1927.

The Aberdeen Corporation bus network grew in the 1930s.
In mileage terms the buses overtook the trams in 1932, but in
passenger terms the trams still carried 13% more — 41.4 million
— in 1939. By the late 1920s, however, the corporation had
accepted that new tramways would not be built to serve developing
areas, the pirate buses having demonstrated that buses could
provide faster services.

In the postwar years the cost of operating the tramway was
growing faster than the income generated, and it was probably
inevitable that buses would replace the trams, as was happening
in other Scottish cities. The Mannofield and Rosemount services
were withdrawn first, leaving just three routes. It was decided that
the tramways would be abandoned by October 1959, although the
rapid deterioration of the track on the Bridges route (No 1, linking
Bridge of Dee and Bridge of Don) meant that final abandonment
was brought forward to May 1958.

Statistics published at the time of the operation of the last tram
show how much the undertaking had grown. In 1899 annual
mileage was 415,087; by 1957 it had grown to 8,015,148.
Passenger figures were equally impressive: 4,110,662 in 1899
and 100,885,626 in 1957. Although mileage rose steadily over
this period, passengers peaked in 1948 at just over 120 million.
The subsequent drop in passengers and the continued growth in
mileage provide a clue to some of the problems that would face
bus operators throughout the UK in the 1960s and beyond.

Built by Aberdeen Corporation on Peckham P35 trucks, there were seven of these cars delivered in 1924/5. No 103 is seen at Woodside terminus, resting before its return trip to the city centre at Market Street. This car lasted to the end of the Aberdeen system in 1958. *Ian Allan Library*

Aberdeen placed 14 'Pilcher' cars from Manchester Corporation in service in 1948/9, including No 52, seen in Union Street in 1950. These cars were built 1930-2 by Manchester Corporation on Peckham P35 trucks.
A. T. Smith

Aberdeen had standardised on AEC and Daimler buses in the late 1930s, and its wartime deliveries were all Daimler CW types. No 152, a 1945 CWD6 with Duple body, is seen in 1950. Similar No 155 is now preserved, restored to its original utility condition.
A. T. Smith

30

The first new electric cars were eight open double-deckers built in 1899 by Brush, and 48 more Brush and British Electric Car (BEC) cars were bought in 1901-3. Between 1912 and 1914 a further 16 cars were bought from various builders.

Between 1918 and 1931 Aberdeen built 41 of its own cars at its Dee Village works. From 1923 these were fully-enclosed trams, as were nine built by Brush in 1925.

All Aberdeen trams had been traditional four-wheelers, but in 1940 the corporation bought four streamlined cars from English Electric. Two were 64-seat four-wheelers, but a second pair were 74-seat bogie cars. Twenty more bogie streamliners followed in 1949, built by Pickering of Wishaw under contract from English Electric. These would be the last new trams built for Aberdeen.

Second-hand cars were bought on two occasions. In 1936 18 English Electric cars built in 1927 were bought from Nottingham Corporation, and in 1948-50 14 1930-built 'Pilcher' cars were purchased from Manchester Corporation.

The first motorbuses bought by Aberdeen Corporation were single-deck Thornycrofts, and this make was chosen until 1926, when an Albion was received. Both Albions and Thornycrofts were bought until 1930, when the first double-deck buses — 14 Crossley Condors with locally-built Walker bodies — were added to the fleet. There were also seven Cowieson-bodied Crossley Arrows. Crossley and Thornycroft double-deckers were bought in 1933, but from 1934 the buying policy changed. That year an AEC Q and two Guy Wolf seaside runabouts were bought, followed in 1935 by 10 more Qs and eight Albion Valkyries, all with Walker bodies.

Like Dundee, Aberdeen then entered a period of standard-isation on AEC and Daimler buses. There were AEC Regals in 1936/7 and Regals and Regents in 1939. After the war there were Regent IIIs in 1946/7 and 1949 and Regent Vs from 1955 to 1959. AEC Swifts were bought in 1968/9 and 1971/2 and Reliances in 1968 and 1970.

Daimler COG5 single-deckers were bought in 1936, and COG6 double-deckers in 1937-9. During the war years CWA6s and

CWG5s were delivered, with CWD6s following in 1945-7. CVD6 single-deckers were bought in 1948, followed by CVG6 double-deckers from 1950 to 1965. Daimler Fleetlines were bought in 1966, 1971 and 1973.

Ten Crossley SD42/7 coaches were bought in 1950, but from 1966 Leylands were increasingly favoured. There were Tiger Cubs in 1966/7, Atlanteans in 1967 and 1973, and Nationals in 1973. A Ford/Alexander S-type midibus was bought in 1974.

Supporting the local economy, Aberdeen chose Walker body-work from 1929 to 1948, but Weymann products were favoured in the 1930s and between 1946 and 1950. During the war, Brush,

▲ In 1946/7 Aberdeen received 15 RT-type AEC Regent III chassis with Weymann bodywork. No 24 travels from the King Street garage to take up a run on route 30.
Stewart J. Brown

▶

Contrasting the Crossley and Metro-Cammell bodies mounted on Aberdeen's 1954 delivery of Daimler CVG6s. No 177 on the left has a 60-seat Crossley body and No 172 an early MCW Orion body. The Crossley-bodied buses weighed 7.5 tons and the Orions 6.75 tons.
Ian Maclean

Duple and Massey bodies were delivered, and in the postwar years Brockhouse and Northern Coachbuilders products were also chosen. Added to the list in the 1950s were Crossley, Metro-Cammell, Park Royal and (in 1959) Alexander, which from 1961 would build all new bodies.

Over the years, Aberdeen Corporation bought its fair share of second-hand buses, including ex-demonstrators in 1931 and 1936 and eight Albion PM28 single-deckers from Glasgow Corporation in 1932. Although it acquired seven buses with the local Rover Bus Service in 1935, it retained just two — AEC Qs. In 1971 it bought four AEC Reliances from Leeds City Transport, and in 1975 six former Greater Glasgow PTE Daimler CVG6/Alexander double-deckers, similar to buses bought by Dundee Corporation at the same time from the same source.

Grampian Regional Transport took over from Aberdeen Corporation on 16 May 1975. The green/cream Aberdeen colours were retained for the Region-owned fleet, but with the effective addition of an orange band.

Aberdeen Corporation operated from a number of depots — at Queen's Cross, Constitution Street, Woodside, Mannofield, Canal Road and Torry — over the years, but most important was the former barracks in King Street, purchased in 1914 and opened as a depot in 1920. The works functions formerly carried out at Dee Village were duly transferred in, and the premises developed until (from 1958) it housed the entire bus fleet. The garage is still used by First Aberdeen, and it is significant that FirstGroup plc has its registered office here. In 1989 Grampian Regional Transport Ltd became the first Scottish council-owned bus company to be privatised, when it was bought by its management and employees. Grampian grew by acquisition and in 1995 merged with Badgerline to create FirstBus, the initial step towards today's First international mega-group.

Exhibited at the 1957 Scottish Motor Show at Kelvin Hall, Glasgow, Aberdeen No 254, an AEC Regent V MD2RA with 66-seat Park Royal bodywork. These would be the corporation's last Park Royal bodies, as from 1961 it turned exclusively to Alexander.
Gavin Booth collection

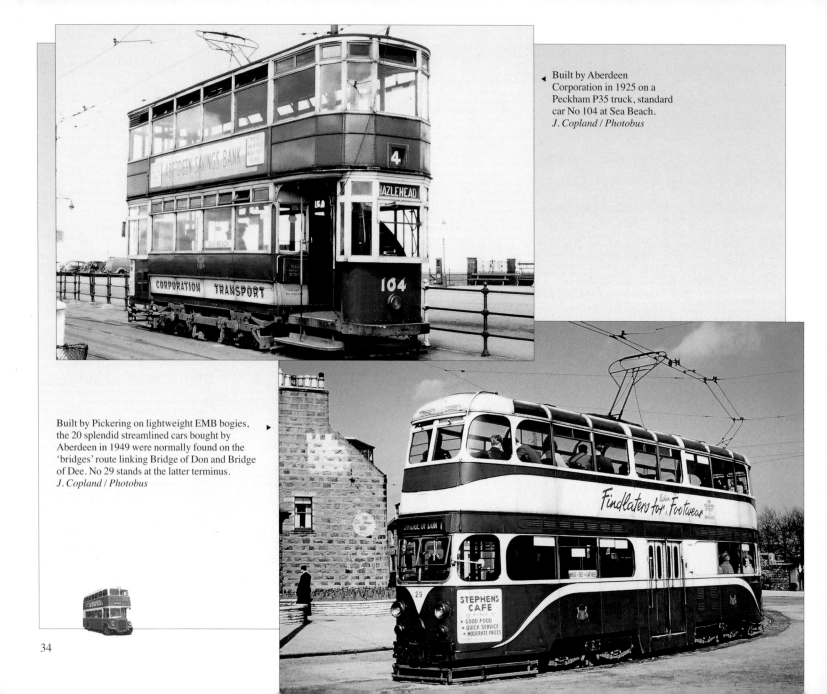

Built by Aberdeen
Corporation in 1925 on a
Peckham P35 truck, standard
car No 104 at Sea Beach.
J. Copland / Photobus

Built by Pickering on lightweight EMB bogies,
the 20 splendid streamlined cars bought by
Aberdeen in 1949 were normally found on the
'bridges' route linking Bridge of Don and Bridge
of Dee. No 29 stands at the latter terminus.
J. Copland / Photobus

▲ Turning from King Street into Castle Street in October 1964 while a policeman apparently pirouettes in the background, Aberdeen No 54, a 1949 AEC Regent III with 56-seat Weymann body. *Iain MacGregor*

◄ Two of Aberdeen's 1947 delivery of Daimler CVD6 single-deckers were rebodied in 1958 with this unique style of Alexander body for use on city tours. The body shows evidence of the contemporary styles usually found on Tiger Cubs or Reliances. No 9 is seen at the Advocates Road works in October 1964 awaiting an Omnibus Society party enjoying a weekend in the North East.
Iain MacGregor

Dual-door Leyland Tiger Cubs were rare, and Aberdeen's six delivered in 1966 were the only examples built with Alexander Y-type bodies. No 5 is working on a tour of the city and suburbs. *John Burnett*

Four AEC Reliance 2MU2RA models were bought by Aberdeen from Leeds City Transport in 1971. They had 41-seat dual-door bodies by Roe. No 44 is seen crossing from Castle Street into Union Street. *Alan Millar*

Aberdeen was the first Scottish municipal fleet to buy the Leyland National when it took three 10.3m-long examples in 1973. No 41 is seen on the 4 route against typical granite suburban housing. *Ian Allan Library*

The last new double-deckers bought by Aberdeen Corporation were Leyland Atlantean AN68/1R models with Alexander AL-type dual-door bodies delivered in 1973. No 160 is seen in Union Street. Grampian continued to buy similar buses for a number of years. *J. G. Carroll*

▲ Aberdeen continued to standardise on conventional 27ft-long rear-entrance double-deckers of this type until 1965. No 300 of 1962, a Daimler CVG6 with Alexander 66-seat body, is seen in Guild Street, adjacent to the city's bus and rail stations. *Campbell Sayers*

▲ At Castle Street in October 1964, a focal point of bus operation in Aberdeen, No 37, a 1951 Daimler CVG6 with Clydebank-built Brockhouse bodywork. Brockhouse, associated with Park Royal, supplied bodies to all four Scottish municipal fleets in the early postwar period, based on Park Royal frames. *Iain MacGregor*

Guild Street again, and No 177, one of the 1954 Daimler CVG6s with distinctive Crossley bodies. The roofs were no longer painted grey by this time, improving the appearance of the green/cream livery. *Photobus*

On a dirty day in September 1974, Aberdeen No 155, a 1973 Leyland Atlantean AN68/1R with AL-type Alexander bodywork. *Gavin Booth*

39

Dundee

For much of the period covered by this book, Dundee vied with Aberdeen to be Scotland's third-largest town, based on population. The saying was that Dundee's prosperity was based on jute, jam and journalism, and certainly these industries were the major employers. About half of the employed people in Dundee worked in the jute mills, and jam (notably marmalade) and journalism (in particular that very Scottish publisher, D. C. Thomson) accounted for a good proportion of the remainder. The jute trade suffered from the growth of new materials and the liberalisation of jute imports, and in recent years new and less-traditional industries — office machinery, electronics and consumer durables — have helped to offset its decline.

Dundee Corporation's first tramway was built in 1877, but because municipalities were not empowered to operate their own tramways it was leased to a newly-created company, Dundee & District Tramways, which began operating horse trams in August 1877.

The new tramway was extended in 1879/80, and authority was obtained for trials with steam traction. Although steam-hauled trams were briefly in vogue at the time, before electric traction became a serious contender, and several systems tried them, few became heavily involved. In Scotland, Edinburgh flirted briefly with steam tram engines, but Vale of Clyde Tramways and Dundee & District made more serious use of steam.

Following experiments with steam haulage in 1880, Dundee & District converted its Lochee route to steam in 1885, with other routes following in 1886. Further routes opened with steam traction in 1894.

As was the practice of the time, Dundee Corporation started to negotiate the purchase of the Dundee & District business, and the corporation took control on 1 June 1899. Following a pattern that was becoming familiar in other parts of the country, the corporation started to electrify the tramway system, the conversion taking place between 1900 and 1902. The last steam trams ran in May 1902.

A network of tram routes was quickly established and would remain relatively unchanged for many years. The shape of the

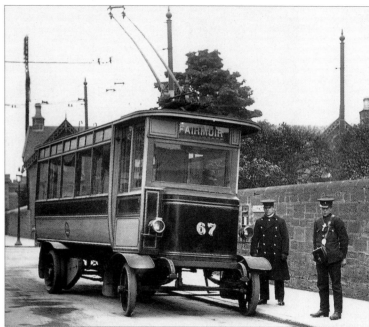

city, with its centre on the north bank of the Firth of Tay, meant that routes radiated out to (from west to east) Ninewells, Balgay, Lochee, Hilltown, Downfield, Maryfield, Baxter Park and Craigie Terrace. At Craigie Terrace, the city's eastern boundary, the Dundee tramways met those of the privately-owned Dundee, Broughty Ferry & District Tramways Co, which from 1905 operated electric cars from Monifieth through Broughty Ferry and into Dundee, jointly with the corporation. But, suffering from deteriorating track and pirate bus competition, the tramway company sold out in 1931 to the corporation, which closed the tramway beyond the boundary and replaced it with motorbuses.

Dundee was Scotland's first trolleybus operator, buying two Railless vehicles in 1912 for a service along Clepington Road, linking the Downfield and Maryfield tram routes. The experiment was not a great success, mainly because of the poor condition of the road surface. The service was discontinued in 1914 and the buses were sold to Halifax. It would be 35 years before trolleybuses ran again in Scotland.

continued on page 47

At Westpark Road, a terminus for short workings on the Blackness route, a 1920 Hurst Nelson car prepares to return to Maryfield. *Photobus*

Dundee's Lochee terminus in the mid-1950s, with No 41, a rebuilt 1920 Hurst Nelson car on EMB truck, ready to return to the High Street. An Alexanders Leyland Tiger PS1 heads north out of the city. *courtesy Alan Brotchie*

Flanked by billboards extolling the virtues of (among others) Duncan's hazelnut chocolate, Isle of Man steamers, beer and Stork margarine, Dundee Corporation No 4 at Downfield terminus in the 1950s. New in 1900, it was one of the corporation's first 10 trams, built by the Electric Railway & Tramway Carriage Works Ltd, and extensively rebuilt in 1930/1 on EMB trucks. They survived until 1955. *Photobus*

An atmospheric 1950 view in Dundee High Street with a later No 32 — a 1926 Dundee Corporation-built car on Peckham P35 truck — and a rebuilt Hurst Nelson car. *A. T. Smith*

The last trams built for Dundee Corporation were 10 Brush cars on EMB trucks delivered in 1930, the 'Lochee cars'. No 24, Lochee-bound, at South Lindsay Street in the early 1950s.
courtesy Alan Brotchie

Dundee Corporation bought 30 ex-London Transport Cravens-bodied AEC Regent III RTs to complete its tram replacement in October 1956. Bus No 220, formerly RT1412, poses alongside 1930 Brush-built Lochee car No 22 at Lochee terminus in the closing months of the system.
Ian Allan Library

Buses are prepared for service at the Central depot in Lochee Road in 1934. Prominent is No 59, a 1932 AEC Regent with Park Royal bodywork, one of three similar buses bought that year. *courtesy Alan Brotchie*

Still in a fairly ornate version of the green/white Dundee Corporation livery, 1950 AEC Regent III No 146 with Barnard bodywork stands at the former city-centre terminal point in Shore Terrace.
Gavin Booth collection

The Balgay tram route was extended to Blackness in 1914, but the system had almost reached its maximum, and, although further extensions were considered, unlike other Scottish cities there would be no further major changes.

The first Dundee Corporation motorbuses appeared in 1921, when four Thornycrofts were bought, but serious bus operation began in 1927 with the purchase of 10 Leyland PLSC1 Lions. Buses were then bought in regular batches. By 1934 there were as many buses as trams in the fleet, and by 1938 there were 88 buses and 60 trams. Dundee, more than the other Scottish municipal operators, embraced buses at an early stage and used them to serve developing areas beyond the reach of the tramways.

Much of Dundee's city centre was depopulated as new housing was built on the periphery, and buses reached out to areas like Douglas, Fintry, Kirkton, St Mary's and Trottick. A bus station had been opened at Shore Terrace in 1933 as the city terminus for all bus routes, but even as early as the 1950s this had become inadequate and entailed unnecessary mileage and journey time as buses crossed the High Street to reach it.

Some idea of the growth of the city and the speed of its expansion beyond the tramway termini is given by these statistics. Between 1884 and 1914 the number of passengers carried on the trams rose from 1.95 million to 19.04 million. By 1934 buses were carrying 15.57 million passengers to the tramways' 21.6 million, and by 1954 the buses were carrying 52.34 million passengers, the trams 30.49 million.

The first tramway abandonments were in the late 1920s / early 1930s, when uneconomic branches were withdrawn, but, in line with many other municipalities, serious attention was given to tramway replacement in the 1950s, and, after an

From 1955 Dundee Corporation standardised on the Daimler CVG6 for its new purchases. Most had MCW bodywork, but the 1956 batch of six had Park Royal bodies, like No 207, seen here in the Seagate. *Photobus*

Weymann built the bodies for Dundee's 1957 batch of 30 CVG6s. The green livery and the dented front panel make No 254, crossing the Seagate from Commercial Street, a rather sorry sight. *Photobus*

▼ By the time these
schoolchildren were drafted in
by the photographer to admire
Dundee Corporation's latest
bus, the livery had changed
to a drab all-over green. The
bus is one of the first batch of
rear-engined vehicles for the
undertaking, a 1964 Daimler
Fleetline CRG6LX with
78-seat Alexander bodywork,
one of 20 bought that year.
courtesy Alan Brotchie

'experimental' withdrawal of the Blackness tram route in 1955, it was decided that the rest of the system should give way to buses. The improved bus service on the Blackness route resulted in an average increase of 10,000 passengers a week during its first six months, compared with the final six months of tramway operation. This sealed the fate of the rest of the tramway system, and the replacement process was completed in under a year, in just two phases. Writing in *The Commercial Motor* in 1957, C. S. Dunbar suggested that the long life of the Dundee trams was not altogether an unmixed blessing. He pointed out that no new cars were bought after 1930, no extension was opened after 1914 and that all new routes since World War 1 were operated by motorbuses. He paid tribute to the tram fleet, which, although it had become antiquated by the 1940s, did a good job, performing remarkably well on Dundee's many hills.

Dundee never operated the modern-style cars that could be found in Aberdeen, Edinburgh and Glasgow. Some of its first electric cars, bought in 1900, were still in service in 1955 — admittedly rebuilt and re-trucked in the early 1930s — and other trams had similarly long lives. The first cars were bought from

Dick, Kerr & Co, and other suppliers included Brush, Hurst Nelson and Milnes. From 1923 Dundee Corporation was given powers to build its own trams, and over the next three years it built nine cars at its Lochee Road workshops. The last new trams for the corporation, bought in 1930, were built by Brush.

The last trams ran in the early morning of 21 October 1956; when it closed, Dundee's was Britain's last totally traditional tramway.

The city of Dundee has long had a history of trade-union militancy, and the transport department occasionally found itself on the wrong side of this. The introduction of one-man operation (OMO) in the 1960s was a notorious example. Ten AEC Reliance single-deckers had been ordered in 1961 for use as OMO buses, but, although the chassis were built in 1962, the Alexander Y-type bodies were not built until 1964, and the buses were stored at Alexander's Falkirk coachworks until they could be put into service in Dundee in 1966.

In the late 1960s there were serious discussions between the state-owned Scottish Bus Group and Dundee Corporation over the possible purchase of the city undertaking by SBG, but these were abandoned in 1970.

The early motorbus fleet had been all single-deck, but in 1931 12 Leyland Titan TD1s were bought to replace the Broughty Ferry trams, and from that time an increasing number of double-deckers was bought; various types were tried, and some former demonstrators purchased, before the undertaking standardised on AECs and Daimlers. Such was the degree of standardisation that the only new buses bought by the corporation between 1935 and 1975 were supplied by these builders.

AEC single-deckers were Qs in 1935/6, Regals in 1947, Regal IVs in 1953/4, Reliances in 1966 and Swifts in 1968. AEC Regent double-deckers were bought regularly from 1936 to 1940 and from 1948 to 1953. Daimler single-deckers were COG5s from 1936 to 1938, CVD6s between 1947 and 1951 and single-deck Fleetlines in 1970. Like Edinburgh and Glasgow, Dundee showed an interest in the potential of high-capacity underfloor-engined single-deckers in the early 1950s, but it did not pursue the standee option; instead it bought a dual-door AEC Regal IV with Alexander body in 1954 and used it for early experiments with OMO.

Daimler double-deckers were COG6s in 1936 and 1939, CWA6s from 1943 to 1945, CWD6s in 1946/7, CVD6s between 1949 and 1953, CVG6s from 1955 to 1960 and Fleetlines from 1964 to 1975.

1958-vintage Metro-Cammell-bodied Daimler CVG6 No 275, with Manchester-style front, leaves the city centre on Perth Road in the rather drab 1960s livery, which later became drabber when the white band was eliminated. *Iain MacGregor*

In 1951 Dundee bought 10 late-model 30ft-long Daimler CVD6s with 39-seat rear-entrance Brush bodies. No 17 is seen in Barrack Road in June 1966. *Iain MacGregor*

49

From the late 1960s Dundee invested in AEC and Daimler single-deckers for one-man operation. No 230, at Shore Terrace, is a 1970 Daimler Fleetline SRG6LX with dual-door Alexander W-type bodywork. It is painted in the two-tone green livery that indicated OMO buses.
M. A. Penn

In 1971/2 Dundee bought four AEC Swifts from Lanarkshire independent Hutchison of Overtown. Two had Alexander W-type bodies, but the two bought in 1972 had Willow-brook bodies, as on No 67, seen in Crichton Street.
Alan Millar

Bodywork was rather less standardised. In the early years Leyland bodies were favoured, as were bodies built locally by Dickson. Then, from the mid-1930s, Cowieson, English Electric, Metro-Cammell, Park Royal and Weymann bodies were bought. During World War 2 utility Brush, Duple, Massey and Northern Counties bodies were allocated, and in the early postwar years, like so many other fleets, Dundee turned to anyone who could supply bodies in a reasonable time — so there were Barnard, Brockhouse, Brush, Metro-Cammell, Northern Coachbuilders and Weymann examples. Dundee bought its first Alexander bodies in 1953/4, and, although it stuck to established suppliers for a few years, from 1960 it bought only Alexander bodies.

Scottish municipal operators were not known for making many second-hand acquisitions, but Dundee did this on several occasions when circumstances required. Six Paisley District trams were bought in 1914 following a fire at Hurst Nelson that destroyed four new cars bound for Dundee. In addition to the demonstrators already mentioned, Dundee bought 10 nine-year-old former London Transport STL-type AEC Regent II/Weymann in 1955, and, to accelerate the programme of tramway withdrawal, a further 30 ex-London Regents were bought in 1956 (for £1,750 each); these were seven-year-old Regent III/Cravens examples from the RT fleet.

Four 1968 AEC Swifts, two with Alexander bodies and two with Willowbrook bodies, were bought from the independent operator, Hutchison of Overtown, in 1971/2.

Right at the end of Dundee Corporation's existence, 22 double-deckers were bought from Edinburgh Corporation and Greater Glasgow PTE. The Edinburgh buses were 15 Leyland Titan PD2/20 with Metro-Cammell bodies, some more than 20 years

old, and the Glasgow buses were Daimler CVG6/Alexander,
originally bought for spares.

The reorganisation of Scottish local government meant that
Dundee Corporation's transport department passed to Tayside
Regional Council on 16 May 1975. A total of 257 buses passed to
the new Tayside undertaking; the oldest included the 15 Leyland
PD2s recently acquired from Edinburgh, while the youngest were
brand-new Fleetlines. A change of senior personnel brought a
change of vehicle policy, and Tayside became noted for its
substantial fleet of Scottish-built Volvo-Ailsa double-deckers.

In the early days, Dundee's trams were painted in a dark red-
brown colour with white relief, but from 1920 new deliveries
were in leaf green/white. Buses were blue/white at first,
changing to green/white in 1934. In the postwar years the livery
was simplified, and the buses became a rather unattractive all-
over green. A darker green was added from 1970 to distinguish

OMO buses, but white relief started to return in the
corporation's final years.

There were three tram depots, at Lochee, Lochee Road
(Central depot) and Maryfield. Buses were first garaged in Craig
Street but moved in 1929 to the Central depot. The Lochee depot
was considered unsuitable for buses, which used the Central and
Maryfield premises after the withdrawal of the trams, but a new
open-air depot was built at Marchbanks in 1961. The Central
depot and works at Lochee Road were replaced in 1972 when the
new Dock Street premises were opened.

Tayside Regional Council chose two shades of blue with white
relief. In 1986 Tayside Public Transport Ltd was set up as an
arm's-length company to continue the TRC operations, and in
1991, in an employee buyout, Taybus Holdings Ltd bought TPT
from the regional council. In 1997 National Express bought
Taybus, and the company now trades as Travel Dundee.

ATS 904

Also at Marchbanks garage,
in June 1962, is Dundee
No 124, a 1949 Daimler
CVD6 supplied new with a
Barnard body but rebodied
by Alexander in 1959. In this
form it would serve Dundee
until 1972. *Iain MacGregor*

Edinburgh

Scotland's historic capital city grew up around the rocky ridge of the Old Town, linking the Castle with the Palace of Holyroodhouse, and spread outwards in the 18th century, when lack of space in the Old Town and concerns about the sometimes insanitary conditions led to the creation of the New Town to the north of what is now Princes Street. A century later the development of the railway system helped the city to grow, but its most spectacular expansion came in 1920, when the boundaries were changed to encompass the port of Leith and many other areas around the city.

The first horse tramway was opened in 1871 by the Edinburgh Street Tramways Co. In 1893 Edinburgh Corporation acquired much of the EST system and leased it to Dick, Kerr & Co, which sub-leased it to the new Edinburgh & District Tramways Co.

Edinburgh is a hilly city, and the Edinburgh Northern Tramways Co was formed in 1884 to operate cable-driven trams; two routes to the north of the city centre opened in 1888 and 1890. ENT passed to the corporation in 1897, and Edinburgh & District continued the cable operation on these routes. Following the granting of a new 21-year lease in 1898, E&D started a programme of converting the horse tramways to cable operation, and this was achieved between 1899 and 1908. The Edinburgh cable tramway was certainly a mechanical marvel, with miles of underground cable driven from power stations around the city, powering the growing tram fleet. Had Edinburgh decided to opt for the new-fangled electric tramways in 1898, just as Aberdeen, Dundee and Glasgow did at around the same time, it might have provided a more satisfactory tramway system in the early years of the last century. As it was, the cable tramways became increasingly unreliable and were something of a laughing-stock locally.

There were 13 main endless cables running at a fixed speed appropriate to the route, the longest being over six miles long. The cable system at its height operated over 25 route miles, and the Edinburgh system was the fourth-largest in the world.

One electric tramway in the city was built between Ardmillan Terrace and Slateford in 1910; previously Leith Corporation and the Musselburgh & District company had started operating electric cars in their areas right to their boundaries with Edinburgh. At Joppa, passengers changed from the Musselburgh electric cars to the city cable cars, while Leith and Edinburgh passengers did the same at Pilrig. The Pilrig situation was the more notorious;

Pilrig is halfway down Leith Walk, still one of the busiest arteries in the city, with massive traffic flows in both directions. The 'Pilrig muddle' was only sorted out in 1922.

The Edinburgh & District lease ran out on 30 June 1919, and Edinburgh Corporation took the system over the following day. Some 200 cable cars and four electric cars ran on 36 miles of track. The first manager was R. Stuart Pilcher, who came to the city from Aberdeen, oversaw the conversion from cable to electric traction and in 1928 went on to become General Manager of the Manchester Corporation undertaking. One of the most famous municipal managers of his generation, he was succeeded by his deputy, F. A. Fitzpayne, previously Manager of the Leith tramways, whose son, Eric, would become well-known as General Manager of Glasgow Corporation Transport.

The corporation started to look urgently at electrification but also introduced its first motorbuses — touring charabancs as well as single-deckers for tramway feeder services and replacements for the two early cable-car routes and the 1910 electric route.

In 1920 Leith reluctantly became part of Edinburgh, and the Leith Corporation tramway system passed into Edinburgh Corporation control.

Electric trams were needed quickly. Between 1922 and 1924 over 100 new cars were introduced to the fleet and 146 new top-deck covers ordered to allow cable cars to be converted to covered-top electric cars. Some of these trams dated originally from 1899, and some of the later cable-car conversions survived until 1947.

Most of the electric cars for the fleet were built by the corporation itself at its Shrubhill Works. From 1922 to 1924, as the cable-electric conversion was underway, a number of cars were bought from outside builders; later, between 1933 and 1935, modern-style cars were bought as replacement of the former cable cars was considered.

Electric services between Edinburgh and Leith started in June 1922, solving the Pilrig problem at a stroke, and the conversion to electric traction was completed almost exactly one year later. The last conversion was the Joppa route, and the new electric service ran beyond the city boundary to Port Seton, jointly with the Musselburgh & District company. This situation lasted until 1928, when the Musselburgh company abandoned its line beyond Levenhall in the face of increasing motorbus competition. Edinburgh Corporation acquired the lines from the city boundary to Levenhall in 1932 and continued to operate in the separate burgh of Musselburgh until 1954.

In the 1920s and 1930s the tramway system grew to serve the expanding city and reached its peak in the late 1930s, with over 47 miles of tramway. It stretched from beyond the city's eastern boundary at Eastfield to the western boundary at Maybury and in the south reached Colinton and Fairmilehead, with further extensions planned but dropped following the outbreak of World War 2. There was an intensive network of services in the Leith area and to the southwest, while those to the north were limited by the Firth of Forth, which marks the city's northern boundary.

Motorbus services, operated by Edinburgh & District, had actually been started by Edinburgh Corporation in 1914, but the outbreak of World War 1 meant that they lasted barely three months. The corporation's own motorbus fleet started in earnest in 1919, first with Leylands and AECs and then with some unsuccessful three-axle Karriers, before moving on to Morris Commercials and Daimlers. Morrises were briefly popular in the early 1930s, but from 1935 until 1939 only Daimlers were bought.

Initially only single-deckers were bought, but in 1922 a former AEC double-deck demonstrator was purchased, and this was followed by four new AEC double-deckers in 1926. The next double-deckers, ECT's first covered-top examples, were Morris Commercials in 1933, but from 1935 new double-deckers were bought on a regular basis.

New trams continued to join the fleet — all covered-top four-wheelers, mostly built by ECT at Shrubhill. The first totally-enclosed car was built in 1929; previously the standard Edinburgh tram had an enclosed platform but open upper-deck balconies. Many of the cars built at this time incorporated the top decks previously fitted to former cable cars, adopting the fleetnumbers of the 'donor' cars.

ECT built its first truly modern car in 1932, and over the next three years it added experimental all-metal cars from English Electric, Hurst Nelson and Metro-Cammell — some with similar styling to ECT's 1932 prototype, others with domed roofs and

55

Two main tramcar designs dominated the Edinburgh Corporation fleet, and all but a handful were built at the undertaking's Shrubhill Works. No 351, built there in 1926 on a Peckham P22 truck, is seen on the North Bridge approaching Princes Street in 1951. Note the distinctive loading-island on the left.
C. Carter

Latterly, the most familiar trams in Edinburgh were the 84 Shrubhill domed-roof 'Standards' built on Peckham P22 trucks between 1934 and 1950. No 223, built in 1939, is seen among other cars in Princes Street in July 1955. This car lasted to the end of the system 16 months later.
Colour-Rail

▲ Similar to the Shrubhill domed-roof 'Standards' but delivered a few months before the first of these appeared in 1934 were three all-metal cars from Hurst Nelson on Maley & Taunton trucks. Compare No 239 at Granton Square with 1935 Shrubhill-built No 157. *I. Davidson / Colour-Rail*

▲ Quite racy by Edinburgh standards were the 23 streamlined cars delivered in 1934/5 from three different manufacturers. No 27, passing Redford Barracks in Colinton Road, was built by Metro-Cammell in 1935 on a Maley & Taunton truck. *Colour-Rail*

'streamlined' front ends. These experiments led to a new ECT-built standard car, of which 84 were built between 1934 and 1950.

During World War 2 ECT faced the same difficulties as other operators; although the city escaped the severe bombing suffered by other centres, notably Clydebank, it had to work hard to maintain services. Between 1941 and 1945 it received just 51 'unfrozen' and utility buses, many of them non-standard, and managed to build nine new standard trams.

After the war a start was made on updating the bus fleet. Although some were Daimlers and broadly compatible with the prewar standard fleet, others introduced new types of chassis and body into the mix. A new Transport Manager, Moris Little, was appointed in 1948, and he would see the undertaking through the controversial replacement of the tram fleet before leaving to take up appointment as Chairman of the Scottish Bus Group in 1963.

The last new tram was completed at Shrubhill in August 1950, just five months after the first tram route was converted to motorbus operation. There had been 11 second-hand 'Pilcher' cars bought from Manchester from 1947 to 1949, providing some

short-term relief after the war, but in 1952 it was decided that the whole tramway system should be replaced by buses. The process started in 1952 and was completed on 16 November 1956, when the last trams operated.

To replace the prewar and wartime bus fleet and invest in new buses to replace the trams, ECT had to buy over 500 new buses in the years 1949-56; in addition there were 60 former London Transport Guy Arabs rebuilt and rebodied by Duple, while 16 of ECT's own Daimlers were rebodied by Alexander. The biggest single type was the Leyland Titan PD2/20 with MCCW Orion bodywork. Three hundred of these were bought, and they quickly became notorious for their spartan finish and lightweight construction — although they confounded critics by giving 20 years' service in some cases.

With the tramway conversion complete, ECT now concentrated on upgrading its sizeable fleet of single-deckers — a legacy of the many low railway bridges that crossed important routes. From 1959 to 1961 it bought 100 new Leyland Tiger Cubs to replace single-deckers, some of which were over 20 years old.

A unique — and, indeed, famous — single-deck bus bought at the same time was No 101, a 36ft-long Leyland Leopard with a three-door Alexander body. Its rear-entrance layout, with a seated conductor, owed much to Continental practice, and, with substantial standing space, it was seen as an alternative to conventional double-deckers. When first tested on a double-deck route it was not regarded as a success, and it was put on to more conventional single-deck duties, eventually being rebuilt as a single-door airport coach; on withdrawal it was bought for preservation and restored to its original 1961 condition. ECT had already dabbled with standee single-deckers in the early 1950s, but passenger resistance caused all of them to be rebuilt to a more conventional layout.

In the 1960s ECT switched to Leyland and Alexander as its sole double-deck bus chassis and body suppliers, and from 1962 until the corporation passed into Lothian Region control in 1975, 500 Alexander-bodied Leylands were bought — 50 Titan PD2s, 75 Titan PD3s, 225 Atlantean PDRs and 150 Atlantean AN68s.

▲ During World War 2 Edinburgh received Bedford, Daimler and Guy utility buses, and after the war it continued to receive utility-type Guy Arab IIs with 6LW engines (for the city's hills) and relaxed Northern Counties bodies. No 85 of 1946 is seen in St Andrew Square in the mid-1950s. *Photobus*

The postwar equivalent of the prewar standard single-decker was a batch of 10 Daimler COG5s with Metro-Cammell bodies, received in 1948/9. No A92 stands on Waverley Bridge in August 1949. *Gavin Booth collection* ▶

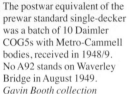

◄ Edinburgh bought a variety of different types of bus in the early postwar period, including 17 of these AEC Regent IIIs with Brockhouse bodies in 1950/1. Decidedly non-standard in the fleet, they were all sold for scrap in 1960. No G236 is seen in St Andrew Square c1950. *C. Carter*

▼ The first substantial batch of postwar double-deckers comprised 72 Birmingham-style Metro-Cammell-bodied Daimlers. All but 10 were CVG6 models, like No 125 seen at Tollcross in September 1959. *J. C. Gillham*

Single-deckers were less of a priority from 1966, when road and bridge alterations removed the low-bridge problem from the busiest single-deck route, allowing 48 of the Tiger Cubs to be sold to the new Ulsterbus concern. The next new single-deck buses were 10 Seddon Pennine IV midis in 1973.

A few words about Edinburgh Corporation's coach fleet. Tourism has always been an important element of the city's economy, and the very first motorbuses bought under full corporation control in 1919 were Leyland charabancs. There were regular deliveries of these until 1921, then three small Dennis charabancs were bought in 1926. Enclosed Dennises were bought in 1928, followed by Morris coaches in 1930 and 1932. These were to be the last new vehicles bought for the coach fleet until 1949, when the first of seven Duple Vista-bodied Bedford OBs arrived; also in 1949 eight utility Bedford OWBs dating from 1942/3 were fitted with similar bodies. The Bedfords constituted the City Tours fleet until 1955, when two Leyland buses, formerly

Edinburgh General Manager Moris Little ordered 16 of these Leyland Royal Tigers with unique rear-entrance Leyland 40-seat bodies, delivered in 1952. No 806 is at Granton Square in April 1953. These buses had been converted to front entrance by 1958, and by 1960 all were in use as coaches in the City Tour fleet. *J. C. Gillham*

Sixteen of Edinburgh's utility Daimlers had their lives extended when new full-fronted Alexander bodies were fitted in 1954; at the same time they were fitted with Gardner 5LW engines in place of the previous 7.7-litre AEC units fitted to all but two of these buses when they were new. No 69, with chassis new in 1944, is seen at the east end of Princes Street. These buses survived until 1967.
Roy Marshall / Photobus

Edinburgh's most famous rebodying programme involved 60 former London Transport utility Guy Arabs bought in 1952 for tram replacement. The chassis were substantially rebuilt and fitted with new 8ft-wide Duple/Nudd full-fronted bodywork. No 320 (originally London Transport G264) is seen in St Andrew Square on the 4 route. The 60 Guys and the 16 rebodied Daimlers all received Leyland-style glassfibre fronts in their later days. *Photobus*

The first batch of Leyland double-deckers for Edinburgh comprised 21 Leyland-bodied PD2/12 Titans delivered in 1952 — the forerunners of a fleet of Titans that would eventually run to some 450 buses. No 251 is seen passing the exit from the Scottish Omnibuses bus station in St Andrew Square. *Photobus*

demonstrators, were rebuilt as coaches, principally for the airport service. Three Leyland Tiger Cub coaches also arrived in 1955, and between 1958 and 1960, 16 Leyland Royal Tiger buses were rebuilt as coaches, replacing the Bedfords.

Another 'odd' single-deck bus, an Albion Aberdonian, was rebuilt as a coach in 1959, but the growing importance of tourism led to the purchase of the first of 65 Bedfords received between 1963 and 1975. There were four VAS, 12 SB, 15 VAL, four VAM, five YRQ and 25 YRT. All but 10 had Duple bodies; the last 10 had Alexander Y-type bodies and were quickly downgraded to buses. There were also two Ford R226 with Duple bodies.

Lothian Region Transport took over in 1975, inheriting a fleet of over 650 buses, including 47 single-deck buses and 45 coaches. The largest single type was the Alexander-bodied Leyland Atlantean, and Lothian continued to buy broadly similar buses for the next six years.

Lothian also continued to use the ECT colours of madder and white, in use since the 19th century on the tramcar fleet. The corporation crest was replaced by the region crest and the legal lettering changed, but externally the city's buses looked little different, unlike those in Aberdeen, Dundee and Glasgow. Not all ECT buses had been madder and white; the prewar coaches had been painted in a bright red, but, although the 1949 Bedfords were in madder and white, they later became black and white after this was adopted for the coach fleet in 1955.

There were electric tram depots at Shrubhill, Leith, Tollcross, Portobello and Gorgie; Shrubhill was mainly used as the tram and later bus works, while the Leith depot was inherited with the Leith Corporation system. The very first buses of 1914 were housed in the Tollcross tram depot, and the 1919 fleet was first garaged at Shrubhill and from 1920 in the former Henderson Row cable car depot. In 1926 a former exhibition hall in Annandale Street was bought, and this became ECT's Central garage. The tram depots at Gorgie, Leith and Tollcross were used to house buses at various times, but by the time Lothian Region took over in 1975 the bus fleet was split between Central, Leith, Longstone (opened 1955) and Marine (1962) garages. Lothian closed the Leith garage in 1977, but the other garages remain in use today with Lothian Buses plc, the corporation's successor. The Shrubhill bus works was closed in 2001.

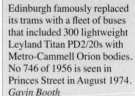

Edinburgh famously replaced its trams with a fleet of buses that included 300 lightweight Leyland Titan PD2/20s with Metro-Cammell Orion bodies. No 746 of 1956 is seen in Princes Street in August 1974. *Gavin Booth*

In addition to the PD2 Orions Edinburgh bought 70 Guys for tram replacement. No 956 of 1956, a Guy Arab IV with 63-seat Alexander body, follows a newer but similarly-bodied Leyland Titan PD2A/30, No 629 of 1962, down Minto Street in March 1967. *Iain MacGregor*

Like Glasgow, Edinburgh dabbled briefly with 30ft forward-entrance buses before moving on to Leyland Atlanteans. No 673, a 1964 Leyland Titan PD3/6, in Princes Street in March 1974, carries a 'broadside' advertisement — a style that was fashionable at the time. *Gavin Booth*

Edinburgh Corporation's elderly single-deck fleet was replaced between 1959 and 1961 by 100 Weymann-bodied Leyland Tiger Cub PSUC1/3 models. No 36 of 1959 is seen descending the Canongate, part of the Royal Mile, in 1964. Forty-eight of these buses, including No 36, were sold to Ulster Transport Authority in 1966, when they became surplus to Edinburgh's requirements following the rebuilding of low bridges on an important route.
Gavin Booth

Princes Street has always been the focal point for Edinburgh's tram and bus services. In this mid-1960s view Leyland Titans of various types tail back from the Mound junction.
Gavin Booth

All but two of Edinburgh's first batch of Leyland Atlanteans, received in 1966, had small-windowed Alexander bodies, similar to contemporary Glasgow buses. All Edinburgh's (and Lothian's) subsequent Atlanteans had panoramic side windows. No 812 turns from Castle Street into Princes Street. *Gavin Booth*

Although Lothian Region Transport would adopt the long-wheelbase Leyland Olympian as standard, Edinburgh Corporation bought just one long Atlantean — this early PDR2/1 with 82-seat Alexander J-type bodywork, No 900, seen at Broomhouse terminus when new. It was the first 33ft Atlantean to enter service in the UK and is now preserved in its later open-top form. *Gavin Booth*

67

▲ Little and large. No 109, a 1973 Seddon Pennine IV.236 Midi, one of 10 bought that year, is passed by Leyland Atlantean PDR1A/1 No 256 of 1971, with dual-door Alexander body. *Gavin Booth*

Unlike Glasgow, Edinburgh (and subsequently Lothian) stuck with dual-door buses for Atlantean deliveries. In Princes Street in August 1974 is No 318, from the first dual-door batch of Alexander-bodied PDR1A/1 models, delivered in 1969. *Gavin Booth*

▶▶

The Glasgow 'Standard' double-bogie cars were better known as Kilmarnock Bogies, after the Kilmarnock Engineering Co maximum-traction bogies on which they were mounted. Between 1927 and 1929, 51 were built by four different manufacturers, including the corporation, which built the two prototypes. In its later years No 1137, built in 1928 by Brush, passes along Argyle Street on the 9 to Dalmuir; these cars were normally confined to the long, straight east–west routes. *Photobus*

'Coronation' No 1181, built in 1938, proceeds eastward along Argyle Street on service 9 to Auchenshuggle — a great name for a tram terminus — having just passed under the Central station bridge, popularly known as the Hielan'man's Umbrella. *Leslie Sandler*

Glasgow

For much of its existence Glasgow Corporation was the UK's largest municipally-owned transport undertaking, running neck-and-neck with Birmingham for that title.

Although depopulation and the growth of Scotland's new towns has caused Glasgow's population to fall well below the magic million mark, it is still an important city and the centre of a conurbation that accounts for nearly half of Scotland's population.

In the early part of the 19th century Glasgow already had a population of 120,000; by 1900 it had grown to over 600,000, and it had hit the 1 million mark by the middle of the 20th century. It was during the Victorian era that Glasgow really came into its own as a centre for shipbuilding and heavy engineering, and the city needed a transport system to match.

Horse buses provided the first local services for the growing population, but in 1870 Glasgow Corporation reached an

agreement with the Glasgow Tramway & Omnibus Co. Under the terms of a 23-year lease granted to the company in 1871, the corporation laid the tracks and the company provided staff and vehicles to operate the services; the corporation would acquire the tramways at the end of the lease.

The first horse-tram route, linking St George's Cross and Eglinton Toll, opened in August 1872, and soon a sizeable network was developed. During the latter part of the lease period, discussions with the company about its renewal broke down, and the corporation resolved to start virtually from scratch and set up its own tramways department; it would use the existing tracks but recruit its own staff, provide its own horses and build depots and tramcars. This it did, and in July 1894 Glasgow Corporation Tramways Department took over the system; John Young, the first General Manager, achieved all of this in the two years following his appointment in 1892.

There was much interest in electric tramways in the last years of the 19th century, and in October 1898 Glasgow started an

experimental service between Mitchell Street and Springburn, using 21 single-deck and four double-deck trams. The double-deckers were the first of over 1,000 'Standard' cars built over the next 26 years, following the corporation's decision to electrify the whole system.

The tramway system grew dramatically. In 1902 there were around 500 electric cars in service; by 1914 there were nearly 1,000.

James Dalrymple succeeded John Young as General Manager in 1904, and over the next 22 years he supervised the development of one of the largest and most successful tramway systems in the country. It was designed to provide cheap fares and an efficient service, and it succeeded on both counts.

Two neighbouring company-owned tramway systems were acquired in the 1920s — Airdrie & Coatbridge in 1921 and Paisley District in 1923 — allowing Glasgow trams to operate well beyond the city boundaries.

A feature of the Glasgow trams until the late 1930s was the absence of route numbers and the reliance on different colours on the panels below the upper-deck windows. These indicated the general directions that the cars would follow beyond the city centre. Route numbers were introduced by 1938, but the colours continued to be worn by the existing trams. New trams from this time would be in what would become the standard livery of cadmium orange, green and cream.

Motorbuses started to appear in the fleet in 1924, when 14 single-deckers of various makes were bought. It would be just four years before buses were purchased in quantity; between 1928 and 1931 Glasgow bought 273 of the newly-launched Leyland Titan TD1, and from 1935 substantial numbers of new buses were delivered. The bus fleet was still outnumbered by the tram fleet, however, and would continue to be for many years yet.

Lachlan MacKinnon was appointed General Manager in 1927 and proceeded to modernise the huge fleet of standard trams, some now nearly 30 years old. He also added the 51 totally-enclosed Kilmarnock Bogie cars in the years 1927-9, and these provided an indication of how future orders would go.

As in the other Scottish cities, the motorbuses were used largely to serve the housing schemes that were being built around the city to accommodate the still-growing population. After the Titan TD1s there were AEC Regents (a type that would figure in the fleet for more than 40 years) and Vulcan Emperors — a rare breed that lasted only eight years in the fleet.

Among the first buses bought by what was now Glasgow Corporation Transport (GCT) were Albion single-deckers, built locally at Scotstoun, but from 1935 Albion double-deckers were purchased, and this make would feature regularly in orders over the next 18 years.

With an increasing requirement for new double-deck buses, GCT multi-sourced its orders in the 1930s, receiving quantities of the Daimler COG6 and Leyland Titan TD4c and TD5, as well as AEC Regents and Albion M81 and CX19 Venturers. The only single-deckers bought between 1928 and World War 2 were seven Albion CX25s in 1939 and 30 AEC Regals in 1940.

Bodywork for the double-deck fleet was first supplied by Leyland on its TD1s but then from 1930 by Cowieson, the Glasgow-based builder, from 1937 additionally by Weymann, and in the last prewar years by English Electric, Metro-Cammell and Pickering.

Between 1928 and 1940 GCT added some 765 double-deckers to its fleet, all from 1935 being diesel-engined.

Built by the corporation on Brill 77E1 bogies in 1926, No 1089 was intended to be the first of a fleet of high-speed inter-urban trams, but, as with many innovations in Glasgow (and elsewhere), it remained unique. Latterly used on shipyard specials from Partick depot, it is seen here in winter sunshine at the other end of the system at Baillieston, Lanarkshire, on a tour organised by the Scottish Tramway Museum Society. It is now preserved in the Glasgow Museum of Transport. *Iain MacGregor*

With the growth of the SMT Group, typically operating longer-distance routes, Glasgow Corporation sought to protect its services, and 1930 legislation gave GCT a monopoly of bus services within the city boundary; SMT Group buses could not pick up or set down passengers travelling wholly within the boundary. The 1930 boundary was not revised when the city expanded outwards in 1938, which would later give other operators a chance to get some lucrative business in the city.

Part of the reason for the investment in new buses was to provide services to the Empire Exhibition held in the city in 1938. Also for 1938 GCT developed a new tramcar, introduced late in 1936 and soon known as the 'Coronation'. These fine streamlined bogie cars were built at the corporation's Coplawhill Works, which had produced most of the famous 'Standard' cars. The 152 'Coronations' built between 1936 and 1941 were part of a plan to build 600 of these trams, but World War 2 interrupted the programme. A Mk II version of the 'Coronation', which would be generally known as the 'Cunarder', was introduced after the war, 100 being built between 1948 and 1952.

By 1938 and the time of the Empire Exhibition there were 27 tram routes operating over 250 track miles. The longest was the 14, which covered an amazing 22·75 miles travelling between Renfrew Ferry and Milngavie.

Although GCT had sought powers to build bus bodies in the 1930s, these were denied. In spite of this, eight double-deck bodies were completed on MCCW frames at Larkfield bus works in 1942; presumably a blind eye was turned in the wartime situation. Powers to build bus bodies were finally obtained in 1946, and GCT used these to build or complete some 173 bodies between 1948 and 1962.

Between 1942 and 1945 Glasgow received 53 Daimler CW and 19 Guy Arab utility double-deckers. It also got a new General Manager, the legendary E. R. L. Fitzpayne. He succeeded Robert Smith in 1943, who had in turn succeeded John Wilson in 1937; Wilson had been appointed when Lachlan MacKinnon had retired in 1935. Eric Fitzpayne would remain in office for 26 years,

becoming one of the best-known and innovative of Britain's municipal managers.

The tramway route mileage reached its maximum of 134·75 in 1949, and in 1952 there were 1,150 cars operating on 32 routes from 11 depots. When London's tramway system closed in 1952, Glasgow became the largest tramway operation in the country.

Glasgow Corporation had investigated trolleybus operation at various stages — in 1921 and 1933 — but after the war the use of trolleybuses to develop new routes and replace some tram routes became a reality. The first Glasgow trolleybus ran in April 1949, and Glasgow's proved to be the last new trolleybus system opened in the UK. New routes were introduced until 1958, but trolleybuses were withdrawn and replaced by motorbuses from 1959, and the system closed in May 1967 after barely 18 years.

Between 1949 and 1959 GCT bought 195 trolleybuses, all but 21 being double-deckers. These were three-axle BUTs and Daimlers with London 'Q1'-style MCCW bodies, two-axle Sunbeams with Alexander and Weymann bodies, and two-axle 30ft-long BUTs with Crossley bodies. The first single-deckers

'Cunarder' car No 1318 crosses the Forth & Clyde Canal by the swing-bridge at Dalmuir, Clydebank, in the last days of Glasgow's trams, on 1 September 1962. It is on the long east–west service 9, which was to be the last tram route on the system. The 100 'Cunarders', strictly 'Coronation' Mk IIs, were built by Glasgow Corporation between 1948 and 1952. No 1318 was new in 1950 and survived to the end of the system. *Leslie Sandler*

No 1398 was the last of six cars built in 1954 to the 1937 'Coronation' design on bogies purchased from Liverpool. They were easily distinguishable from the original 'Coronations' by the rubber glazing and absence of cab doors. *Photobus*

1939-built Glasgow
'Coronation' car No 1240
at the Springburn terminus of
services 18/18A in Hawthorn
Street in May 1961.
Springburn was a major
railway manufacturing
and repair centre even in
the 1960s, but the area
is now totally redeveloped.
Iain MacGregor

◄ Round-dash 'Standard' car
No 779 in Dalmarnock Road
in the Last Tram Procession
on 4 September 1962, during
a brief dry interval before the
heavens opened. First built in
1900, it had been rebuilt with
open platforms to represent an
early phase in the life of these
cars, which went through
many modifications in their
long lives. Both it and the
following No 1088 are now
in the Museum of Transport
at Kelvin Hall, along with
other cars which formed the
procession. *Iain MacGregor*

were 11 BUTs with Weymann (1) and East Lancs (10) bodies. Like Moris Little, his opposite number (and close friend) at Edinburgh, Eric Fitzpayne was keen to test the latest ideas from the Continent, where standee single-deckers with a small seating capacity were seen to be useful crowd-movers. The BUT single-deckers of 1950 and 1953 had dual-door 26- or 27-seat bodies with rear entrances and front or centre exits, but they were rebuilt as more conventional single-door buses within a few years.

The only other single-deckers were equally notable — 10 BUT/Burlinghams built to a length of 34ft 6in under special dispensation at a time when 30ft was the legal maximum.

New buses in the early postwar years were a mix of AEC Regent III (265), Albion CX19 (48) and CX37 (90), and Daimler CWA6 (9) and CVD6 (87) double-deckers, plus a couple of oddments — a Crossley DD42 and a Daimler CD650. There were also 43 Daimler CVD6 single-deckers with bodies built at Larkfield on Metal Sections frames. Two other odd single-deckers were both underfloor-engined — one of only two Albion KP71NW built and a Daimler Freeline.

Bodywork for the double-deckers was bought wherever GCT could get it, so there were Alexander, Brockhouse, Brush, Croft, Crossley, Duple, Mann Egerton, MCCW, Northern

Coachbuilders, Roberts, Scottish Aviation and Weymann bodies delivered between 1946 and 1953.

Glasgow was expanding rapidly in the postwar years as inner-city slums were demolished and their residents re-housed in vast, sprawling new estates built on greenfield sites on the fringes of the city. Areas like Castlemilk, Drumchapel and Easterhouse were developed in the 1950s with little other than housing, so their residents had to travel to the shops, cinemas and pubs. As these developments were beyond the 1930 monopoly boundary, the local Scottish Bus Group companies also obtained licences to operate services into these areas. The SBG companies also benefited from GCT's decision to transfer services that operated beyond the boundary, so in the years 1955-7 GCT's services in the Airdrie/Coatbridge, Clydebank, Milngavie and Paisley areas passed into SBG control.

The abandonment of the once-massive Glasgow tramway system was now well underway, and the new breed of motor-buses introduced from 1955 marked the return of Leylands to the fleet. AEC Regent V, Daimler CVG6 and Leyland Titan double-deckers became standard from that year, some with Weymann bodies, though increasingly Alexander bodies were chosen. Single-deckers had never figured greatly in the GCT

badges incorporating the oval Albion badge as a nod to local industry, but the chassis were built at Leyland, Lancashire.

The last six trams built at Coplawhill had been prewar-style 'Coronations' placed in service in 1954, but in the years 1953-5 GCT bought 46 'Green Goddess' bogie cars from Liverpool, which helped to update the fleet. The once-ubiquitous 'Standard' cars were the first casualties in the tram-replacement programme, but some, remarkably, lingered on in regular service into the 1960s. The last trams ran in September 1962 — the final chapter in a long and proud history of tramway operation in the city, and the last of the 'first generation' street tramways in the UK, leaving only Blackpool with its seaside tramway.

Larger single-deck buses were added to the fleet between 1965 and 1969 in the shape of 36ft-long Leyland Panthers, but these were not successful. They were used to introduce one-man-operated services, but OMO double-deck services were legalised from 1966 and GCT introduced these using Atlanteans in 1968.

The whole future of GCT — and, indeed, in the whole Glasgow area — was now under consideration. There was the Greater Glasgow Transportation Study of 1964, involving road and rail operators and local authorities. There was also the deal that was nearly concluded whereby SBG would have been granted a lease to operate the city's buses. But by the end of the 1960s the first Passenger Transport Authorities (PTAs) had been set up, in the Birmingham, Liverpool, Manchester and Newcastle conurbations, and it seemed inevitable that Glasgow would have its own PTA. The policy-forming Greater Glasgow PTA was set up in 1972 and the Passenger Transport Executive (PTE) in June 1973, taking over Glasgow Corporation Transport Department.

Glasgow's trams were cadmium orange and cream with, at various times, different colours applied to the upper panelling. The route-colour system meant that the orange could be matched with red, blue, white, green or yellow, but, following the intro-duction of route numbers from 1938, the route colours gradually gave way to standard bus green. The 'Coronation', 'Cunarder' and 'Green Goddess' trams entered service in these colours, except for one of the prototype 'Coronations', which was in patriotic red, silver grey and blue to mark King George VI's Coronation in 1937, the year it was built — giving rise to the 'Coronation' name applied to the class. The prototype Mk II 'Coronation' was a unique single-ended car, painted in three shades of blue.

The motorbus livery was basically green, orange and cream, applied in many different styles. From 1959 a simpler version, using large expanses of light green and yellow relieved by a cream

▲ A taste of the excellent standards achieved by Glasgow Corporation employees at Larkfield Bus Works, even during wartime. This 1941 view shows the finishing touches being added to a repaint of No 573, a 1938 AEC Regent with Weymann bodywork. Visible beyond the Regent are Albions and Leylands. *Ian Allan Library*

fleet, but delivered from 1956 to 1958 were 30 rare Leyland Royal Tiger Worldmasters with GCT bodies built at Coplawhill on Weymann frames.

Two odd double-deckers at this time were to the recently-legalised 30ft maximum length. One was a Daimler CVD6-30, but the other was a type that would be synonymous with Glasgow for the next 40 years — the Leyland Atlantean. GCT received one of the four pre-production prototypes built in 1958, and LA1 was followed by significant batches from 1962 onwards, right to the end of the corporation's existence. All had Alexander bodies. Other 30ft double-deckers bought in the meantime were Leyland Titan PD3s and further AEC Regent Vs. Twenty-five of the PD3s had bodies built to Alexander design by GCT at Coplawhill in 1961/2, as did 75 Titan PD2s built between 1958 and 1961. The PD3s would be the last GCT-built bodies. The Leyland PD3s and many of the subsequent Atlanteans had Leyland Albion

In the postwar years Glasgow Corporation had a number of prewar and wartime double-deckers rebodied to extend their lives. Thirty utility Daimler CWA6s received new East Lancs bodies in 1954; DR23, new in 1945 with a Brush body, lasted in service until 1962. *Photobus*

Between 1948 and 1952 Glasgow bought 43 Daimler CVD6s and bodied them in the Larkfield Bus Works in a style similar to that of the contemporary 'Cunarder' tramcars. DS20, new in 1950, is seen on private-hire duties in Renfield Street. *Photobus*

Weymann-bodied AEC Regent III A205 of 1951 leaves
Castlemilk and heads briefly into open country to reach
Carmunnock, high above the city. This route was taken
over by Glasgow Corporation on the death of the previous
operator, Stephen Young of Carmunnock, in 1941 —
the only such incidence in the corporation's history.
Between 1948 and 1952 Glasgow bought 265 Regent IIIs,
including 100 of this type. *Iain MacGregor*

In the postwar years Glasgow supported Albion, with
orders for 138 double-deck chassis. B81, a Roberts-bodied
Venturer CX37S new in 1950, is seen in George Square
on a short working of the original Glasgow Corporation bus
route. Both it and the MCW-bodied Regent behind are in the
1959 livery of green and yellow. *Iain MacGregor*

Wearing one of many variations of livery which occurred in the early 1960s, when buses in green, cream and orange received partial repaints in the new shades, D208 was one of 100 Daimler CVG6s with preselector gearboxes and typical Alexander bodywork of the late 1950s. It is returning to the city on Braidcraft Road in Pollok amidst postwar housing. Broomielaw, under the approaches to Glasgow Central station, was the terminus for many South Side services. *Iain MacGregor*

band, was introduced to aid spray-painting. The trolleybuses were originally green, orange and cream applied in a distinctive style; this was simplified from 1953, and the motorbus livery was adopted from 1960.

Glasgow Corporation's trams and buses worked from a bewildering number of depots and garages over its 79-year history. Some 30 premises were used at various times, but in more recent years the trams lived at nine depots spread around the city. Some doubled as bus garages at various stages, and several became bus garages when the tramway system closed. The corporation also opened purpose-built new bus garages from the late 1920s right through to the mid-1960s. Eleven bus garages were transferred to the new PTE in 1973, but several of these were fairly speedily closed by the PTE, and today only three — Knightswood, Larkfield and Parkhead — survive with First Glasgow.

The trolleybuses were mainly housed in Hampden garage, opened in 1950, but others were stabled at Dennistoun and Govan.

The tramcar works was at Coplawhill, which closed after the end of tramway operation; the bus works was at Larkfield.

Some 1,318 buses were taken over by the PTE in 1973 — AEC, Daimler and Leyland double-deckers (including nearly 700 Atlanteans) and 16 Leyland Panther single-deckers. The PTE continued the corporation's Atlantean/Alexander policy, taking the city's fleet of these to nearly 1,450 examples, but Ailsa, Metropolitan, Metrobus and Olympian double-deckers would subsequently be bought.

Photographed when brand-new in 1949, Glasgow BUT 9641T trolleybus TB2 with 70-seat Metro-Cammell body is clearly derived from London Transport's famous 'Q1' class, right down to the Trolleybus symbol on the front panel — later removed, following protests from London!
Ian Allan Library

Glasgow Corporation obtained special permission to buy 10 of these BUT RETB1 trolleybuses with 34ft 6in-long Burlingham bodies in 1958, when the maximum legal length was still 30ft. They were bought for the 108 route — the last tram-trolleybus conversion in Britain, which began in November 1958. These buses are thought to have paved the way for 36ft-long buses and coaches, legalised in 1961. TBS13 was shown by BUT at the 1958 Commercial Motor Show at Earls Court in the company of TB107 (right). *Ian Allan Library*

Glasgow's only two-axle double-deck trolleybuses were 20 Sunbeam F4 models bought in 1953. TG5 has a 62-seat Alexander body — one of five built at Stirling. These were Alexander's first trolleybus bodies and, indeed, the only ones until South Yorkshire's experimental Dennis Dominator, built more than 30 years later.
Ian Allan Library

Glasgow's first trolleybuses were 34 Metro-Cammell-bodied BUTs to London's 'Q1' design but with Glasgow destination indicators bought to open the system in 1949. TB22 passes old factories and new houses on Rutherglen Road on the last day of the 101 route, 30 April 1966, having succumbed to the 'new' bus livery. *Iain MacGregor*

The largest batch of trolleybuses were the 90 BUT 9613T models with Crossley bodies to Park Royal design (and recent evidence suggests most were, in fact, built at Park Royal) delivered 1957-9. TB120 is seen heading for Muirend on the 103 route. Trolleybus liveries varied with type and time but until the 1960s were usually different in layout from those on motorbuses. *Campbell Sayers*

D266 was numerically the penultimate Daimler CV to join the Glasgow fleet (in 1959) and was one of five which when new were fitted with turbocharged Daimler CD6 Mk VIII engines and Daimatic transmission; all received more standard Gardner 6LW engines in the early 1970s. It is in Shawlands on one of the busy services from the city centre to the Pollok housing scheme. *Iain MacGregor*

A 1962 AEC Regent V with Alexander body, A426, crosses the Clyde by Victoria Bridge. These 89 Regents, delivered between 1960 and 1962, were originally intended to have Gardner engines like those of the 1955 batch, but they came with AV590 engines and semi-automatic transmission. All of Glasgow's Regent Vs had plain slotted radiator grilles rather than the normal AEC design. *Iain MacGregor*

◄ Nearly 300 Leyland Titan PD2/24 models were bought by Glasgow Corporation between 1956 and 1960. All had bodies to this design, though 75 were built by the corporation at its Coplawhill Works. The rest, like L309 seen when new crossing Argyle Street, had Alexander bodies. It provides a good example of Glasgow's apparent disregard for matching fleet and registration numbers: frustratingly, L309 is SGD 311. *Photobus*

◄ From Leyland Titan PD2s Glasgow passed on to the 30ft-long PD3/2, placing 140 in service between 1960 and 1962, all with Alexander or Alexander-style GCT forward-entrance bodies. Alexander-bodied L398, with almost-matching registration number, was the sole PD3A/2 with glassfibre St Helens-style front. It is seen in 1971 in Parliamentary Road, outside the Dundas Street bus station of Alexander (Midland). *Alan Millar*

Between 1959 and 1964 Glasgow Corporation took no single-deckers, but in 1965 it bought a Leyland Panther, followed by another in 1966, yet another in 1968 and 13 more in 1969. This is the 1968 example, LS33, with dual-door Alexander W-type body. *Gavin Booth*

Despite having a considerable fleet of front-engined Daimlers, Glasgow Corporation had only one Daimler Fleetline, new in 1963. The Leyland Atlantean ruled. Like all solitary vehicles, D268 led an unhappy existence for 12 years or so until it was allowed to mix with more of its own breed with Graham's of Paisley. *Iain MacGregor*

Glasgow Corporation built up a fleet of nearly 700 Leyland Atlanteans between 1958 and 1973, and its successors went on to buy over 700 more. LA548, seen at St Enoch Square in 1971, is a PDR1A/1 delivered that year with dual-door Alexander J-type bodywork. Although dual-door double-deckers were standard from 1968, Glaswegians were notoriously unwilling to use the centre exit, and Greater Glasgow PTE reverted to single-door buses in 1974. *Edward Shirras*

The AN68 Atlanteans
introduced the AL-type
Alexander body to the fleet.
Centre exit doors never found
favour in Glasgow and were
eventually removed. LA696
is in full Glasgow Corporation
livery, although it was actually
delivered to the newly-
established Greater Glasgow
PTE, in June 1973; this rare
pre-repaint view is in
Sauchiehall Street.
Alan Millar

Right at the end of its existence,
Glasgow Corporation tried
this Volvo B59 demonstrator
with Marshall Camair
bodywork on its 39 service.
It was the only B59 to
operate in the UK.
Gavin Booth collection

Glasgow Corporation's other electric transport system was the
Underground (known popularly as the subway), opened in 1896
as a cable-driven circular 4ft-gauge railway and electrified in 1923.
One of the distinctive cars, built in 1896 by the Oldbury Railway
Carriage & Wagon Co, is seen at a typical narrow island platform.
Photobus

Lothian Region Transport continued Edinburgh Corporation's purchasing policy, adding further batches of Alexander-bodied Atlanteans like No 579 of 1979, seen here in Bank Street. Just visible above the crest on the side is a gold LOTHIAN transfer, a short-lived addition to the livery before more prominent Lothian badging was adopted in 1986.
Gavin Booth

There was little external change to the Edinburgh Corporation fleet after it passed into Lothian Region control. The madder-and-white colours and their application were unchanged, and only the crest and legal lettering showed that there had been a change of ownership. Initially it was a simple label-sticking exercise; this newly-delivered Alexander-bodied Atlantean shows the vinyls that have been stuck over the corporation crest and address. The photograph was taken on 15 May 1975 — the last day of corporation control.
Gavin Booth

EXIT ONLY

LOTHIAN REGION, TRANSPORT DEPARTMENT, 14 QUEEN STREET, EDINBURGH, EH2 1JL

Today only one of the four big Scottish municipal fleets remains in council control — Lothian Buses PLC, with the City of Edinburgh Council as the major shareholder (91.01%) and the rest divided between East Lothian, Midlothian and West Lothian councils. Many of the buses still look very traditional and municipal, painted in the long-standing madder/white colours, although low-floor buses wear a more modern scheme that still includes madder and white, along with gold and a bright red. The Lothian route system is still identifiably based on the tramway system at its height in the early postwar years, although the size and population of the city have grown and many of the services operate beyond the boundary into East Lothian and Midlothian in a way they never could in corporation days, a consequence of deregulation.

There are fewer traces of the other three former municipal bus and tram undertakings. Some still use premises that were in use in corporation days, but corporate liveries have long since replaced more familiar colours on the buses.

In Aberdeen green remained an important ingredient in the livery of the city's buses (although the shades had changed) right through the Grampian period into FirstGroup days, but that has been swept away in favour of First's 'Barbie' liveries.

In Glasgow too the buses went through various green/yellow liveries, including some with white relief and some with black, before the infamous 'Strathclyde Red' (actually orange) replaced these — and, just when observers thought the orange was drab and uninspired, First Glasgow came along with an even less inspired all-red scheme. Glasgow's buses are also being 'Barbie-ised'.

Dundee's drab latter-day green gave way to a more modern blue/white livery under Tayside, and this was developed with cream relief replacing the white. Now under National Express ownership, Dundee's buses wear an attractive white/red/blue scheme based on that worn by the vast fleet of its southern big brother, Travel West Midlands.

Of the five municipal fleets that disappeared in the 1930s there is little trace of four, except that a few of the bus routes operated by the present-day successors (Stagecoach in Ayr, Kilmarnock, Kirkcaldy and Perth) can be traced back to tram days. At Leith, Edinburgh Corporation essentially won back routes it had developed in horse-bus days and added these to its own services

Canonmills
Mound
Tollcross

27

SILVERKNOWES

P&O TRAVEL

031-225 5373   30 GEORGE ST EDINBURGH

PACKAGE HOLIDAYS
LOW COST AIR FARES
BUSINESS TRAVEL SERVICE

ATLANTEAN

JSX 579T

▶

Grampian Regional Transport simply added an orange band to the Aberdeen livery and continued to buy standard dual-door Atlanteans with Alexander bodies until 1983. This 1978 example is seen in Union Street. *Gavin Booth*

when these were electrified in 1922/3; some of these routes are very recognisably the same.

Scotland was well served by its municipal tram and bus fleets, which provided a high quality of service using vehicles that were generally attractive and well-maintained. In corporation days such standards came at a price, for staff numbers were high at a time when part of the *raison d'être* of transport departments was to provide local employment. This has meant that the successors to the corporation transport departments have had to bite the

bullet on a number of issues by introducing driver-only operation, closing the massive central workshops that were inherited and drastically reducing a workforce that could (and did) turn its hand to virtually anything — look at all those 'home-made' tramcars. These have been unpopular and uncomfortable decisions for new management, and there are still generous conditions in place as a result of the more benevolent attitude adopted by municipal employers as compared with the more down-to-earth local SMT/SBG companies.

Tayside Regional Council moved away from the drab Dundee greens, adopting an attractive livery of two shades of blue with white, and immediately moved away also from the predominantly Daimler fleet with substantial purchases of the new Volvo-Ailsa front-engined double-decker. Although most had Alexander bodies, this 1983 example has 84-seat East Lancs bodywork.
Gavin Booth

Glasgow's Victorian Underground system closed in May 1977 for modernisation, a process that was completed with its re-opening with new stock in April 1980. Greater Glasgow PTE provided replacement bus services during the closure. Leyland Atlantean/ Alexander LA1020 of 1976 stands at Kelvinbridge Underground station on the 101 Inner Circle service in 1977, wearing the PTE's original livery of green, yellow and white with 'GG' logo.
Alan Millar

At the time Greater Glasgow PTE was changing its name to Strathclyde PTE, in 1980, a revised livery was introduced using the same green and yellow colours but with (mainly on Atlanteans) a white band or (on most other types) black window surrounds and skirt. This looked effective on modern types like the 30 low-height ECW-bodied Leyland Olympians bought in 1982/3, of which LO23 is seen crossing from Jamaica Street to Glasgow Bridge in 1983. It carries the Trans-Clyde logo adopted at this time. *Gavin Booth*

It was rare for Lothian and Strathclyde buses to be seen side by side, but in Leith, Edinburgh, in 1981 a 1975 Lothian Leyland Atlantean AN68/1R was photographed passing a similar Strathclyde bus dating from 1974 which was in the city on private-hire work.
Gavin Booth

Further Reading

Many publications produced over the years have dealt with Scotland's municipal tram and bus fleets. These are the books I found most useful in preparing this book, although many are no longer in print. I have listed the publisher, the author(s) and the date published, where known.

Aberdeen Corporation Transport Department:
Sixty Years of Progress (1958)
Adam Gordon:
Edinburgh's Transport — The Corporation Years (D. L. G. Hunter, 1999)
Dundee Museum & Art Gallery:
Tramways of the Tay Valley (Alan W. Brotchie, 1965)
First Aberdeen Ltd:
Fae Dee to Don and Back Again (Mike Mitchell, 1998)
Ian Allan Ltd:
abc British Bus Fleets 20: Glasgow Corporation Transport (Ian Maclean, 1963),
British PTEs 1: Strathclyde (Alan Millar, 1985)
Light Rail Transit Association:
The Tramways of Eastern Scotland (J. C. Gillham and R. J. S. Wiseman)
NB Traction:
Scottish Tramway Fleets (Alan W. Brotchie, 1968), *Aberdeen's Trams 1874-1958* (H. R. MacKenzie and A. W. Brotchie),
Kilmarnock's Trams and Buses (A. W. Brotchie and R. L. Grieves, 1984),
The Tramways of Kirkcaldy (Alan W. Brotchie, 1978),
Dundee on the Move, 1877-1977 (A. W. Brotchie and J. J. Herd, 1977)

PSV Circle/Omnibus Society Fleet Histories:
Aberdeen Corporation Transport succeeded by Grampian Regional Transport, *Dundee Corporation Transport succeeded by Tayside Regional Council*, *Perth Corporation Transport* (PL1, 1977),
Edinburgh Corporation Transport succeeded by Lothian Region Transport (PM1, 1977),
Strathclyde Passenger Transport Executive (PM11, 1985),
Glasgow Corporation Transport (PM12, 1986)
Scottish Tramway Museum Society:
Glasgow's Tramways (Ian L. Cormack),
Tramways of the Monklands (Ian L. Cormack, 1964),
Tramways of Scotland (Ian L. Cormack),
Glasgow Trams Beyond the Boundary (Ian L. Cormack, 1967),
A Handbook of Glasgow Corporation Motorbuses 1924-1971 (Stuart M. Little, 1972),
Almost 50 . . . But Not Quite! (Stuart Little, 1974),
Glasgow's Trolleybuses (Brian T. Deans, 1977)
Scottish Tramway & Transport Society:
The Glasgow Tramcar (Ian G. McM. Stewart, 1994)
The Glasgow Museums & Art Galleries Dept.:
Glasgow Corporation Motor Buses — An Historical Survey (1969)
Transport Publishing Co/STTS:
Glasgow Buses (Stuart Little, 1990)
XS Publications:
Glasgow Bus Scene (Robert Grieves, 1981),
Glasgow's Trams and Buses — A Centenary Journey (Robert Grieves, 1994)